I0410611

BEYOND BIN LADEN'S CAVES AND COURIERS TO A NEW GENERATION OF TERRORISTS: CONFRONTING THE CHALLENGES IN A POST-9/11 WORLD

FIELD HEARING

BEFORE THE

COMMITTEE ON HOMELAND SECURITY
HOUSE OF REPRESENTATIVES

ONE HUNDRED FOURTEENTH CONGRESS

FIRST SESSION

SEPTEMBER 8, 2015

Serial No. 114–31

Printed for the use of the Committee on Homeland Security

Available via the World Wide Web: http://www.gpo.gov/fdsys/

U.S. GOVERNMENT PUBLISHING OFFICE

99–573 PDF   WASHINGTON : 2016

For sale by the Superintendent of Documents, U.S. Government Publishing Office
Internet: bookstore.gpo.gov   Phone: toll free (866) 512–1800; DC area (202) 512–1800
Fax: (202) 512–2104   Mail: Stop IDCC, Washington, DC 20402–0001

COMMITTEE ON HOMELAND SECURITY

MICHAEL T. McCAUL, Texas, *Chairman*

LAMAR SMITH, Texas
PETER T. KING, New York
MIKE ROGERS, Alabama
CANDICE S. MILLER, Michigan, *Vice Chair*
JEFF DUNCAN, South Carolina
TOM MARINO, Pennsylvania
LOU BARLETTA, Pennsylvania
SCOTT PERRY, Pennsylvania
CURT CLAWSON, Florida
JOHN KATKO, New York
WILL HURD, Texas
EARL L. "BUDDY" CARTER, Georgia
MARK WALKER, North Carolina
BARRY LOUDERMILK, Georgia
MARTHA McSALLY, Arizona
JOHN RATCLIFFE, Texas
DANIEL M. DONOVAN, JR., New York

BENNIE G. THOMPSON, Mississippi
LORETTA SANCHEZ, California
SHEILA JACKSON LEE, Texas
JAMES R. LANGEVIN, Rhode Island
BRIAN HIGGINS, New York
CEDRIC L. RICHMOND, Louisiana
WILLIAM R. KEATING, Massachusetts
DONALD M. PAYNE, JR., New Jersey
FILEMON VELA, Texas
BONNIE WATSON COLEMAN, New Jersey
KATHLEEN M. RICE, New York
NORMA J. TORRES, California

BRENDAN P. SHIELDS, *Staff Director*
JOAN V. O'HARA, *General Counsel*
MICHAEL S. TWINCHEK, *Chief Clerk*
I. LANIER AVANT, *Minority Staff Director*

CONTENTS

BEYOND BIN LADEN'S CAVES AND COURIERS TO A NEW GENERATION OF TERRORISTS: CONFRONTING THE CHALLENGES IN A POST-9/11 WORLD

Tuesday, September 8, 2015

U.S. HOUSE OF REPRESENTATIVES,
COMMITTEE ON HOMELAND SECURITY,
New York, NY.

The committee met, pursuant to call, at 9:00 a.m., in Foundation Hall, National September 11 Memorial & Museum, New York City, New York, Hon. Michael T. McCaul [Chairman of the committee] presiding.

Present: Representatives McCaul, King, Miller, Clawson, Katko, Hurd, Ratcliffe, Donovan, Sanchez, Jackson Lee, Vela, and Rice.

Chairman MCCAUL. The Committee on Homeland Security will come to order.

Before we begin, I would like to introduce Joe Daniels, the president and CEO of the National September 11 Memorial & Museum. Joe.

Mr. DANIELS. Good morning. Thank you, Chairman McCaul, and thank you to all the committee Members for being here this morning and choosing to hold this field hearing at this location.

This is the very first time we are hosting such an event at the National September 11 Memorial & Museum. I, on behalf of the organization, our board of directors, and the hundreds of thousands of people who worked to make this place a reality, thank you for your support and, perhaps more importantly, your steadfast commitment by the members of this committee in working to secure the safety of our Nation, which is especially profound given our current location at the very foundations where the towers once stood.

I had the honor of giving some of you a tour of the space last night, and I think we can all agree that this site holds great importance with regard to the topics that will be discussed this morning.

I would also like to thank some of our partner organizations who are here in attendance, including Tuesday's Children, the 9/11 Tribute Center, along with representatives from the September 11 Education Trust and 9/11 Health Watch.

It is of course fitting and appropriate to acknowledge that in just a few days the memorial will host, once again, the solemn ceremony marking the anniversary of the attacks, this year the 14th anniversary. This anniversary is of course significant for all of us, for the entire Nation, but particularly for the victims' families as

(1)

well as the first responders, the recovery workers, survivors, and all others impacted by the attacks, including those who are still dealing with the lingering and devastating health effects so many years later.

On the 10th anniversary, just 4 years ago this week, we opened the memorial, and since then we have welcomed over 21 million visitors from every State in the country and 175 countries around the world, making this one of the most visited historical sites in our country. Just last year, we opened this museum with a dedication ceremony here in this Foundation Hall and have seen a tremendous outpouring of positive feedback. In just over a year, we have welcomed more than 3½ million visitors to the museum.

In addition to the general public, we have had visitors from across the political, cultural, and military spectrum. But for every visit from Prince William and the Duchess of Cambridge and various heads of state, the most meaningful visits have been from the nearly 75,000 active military and veterans, including three recent Medal of Honor winners; the former U.S. Army Chief of Staff Ray Odierno, along with several four-stars from his team; and, last September, we had the entire corps of West Point cadets on the 9/11 Memorial.

Later this month and in this very room where we are sitting right now, we will host one of the most important and beloved figures in the world. Pope Francis will lead a multi-religious meeting for peace, speaking about the idea of what unites us being stronger than what divides. A group of religious leaders will be with him that represent all of the world's major religions.

This memorial and museum not only serves as a place for people from all walks of life to visit and pay their respects but also as a place where future generations will learn about what happened that day, what led up to that day, and the increasingly complex state of world affairs. Let's not forget that children now entering high school were born after 9/11/2001, and, for them, we risk that 9/11 is simply a historical fact. It is to this institution where thousands of educators bring their students every single year to learn the full history of 9/11.

That is why I would like to thank Chairman McCaul, Representatives King and Jackson Lee for already being co-sponsors of the bill H.R. 3036, the National 9/11 Memorial at the World Trade Center Act, which would designate the above-ground beautiful memorial as a true National memorial. Those beautiful pools will ensure that this place is here to preserve the memory of those who were killed and will make sure that we fulfill our obligation to educate future generations.

I would very, very much encourage from the bottom of my heart that all Members of this committee, this incredibly important committee, support H.R. 3036, as this is a momentous opportunity to take the lead in preserving the memory of one of the most important events in the entire history of the United States.

This memorial has truly become not only the location to remember and educate but is the physical embodiment of the unity, the coming together, that was so prevalent in the aftermath of the attacks.

Thank you for your time here today and for your continued support.

Chairman MCCAUL. Well, thank you, Joe. On behalf of the committee, let me thank you for your dedication, your service to the victims and their families. Let us never forget, and may it never happen again.

I was inspired at our dinner last night to hear from you and your efforts. I am proud to be a co-sponsor of the legislation that you talked about.

Again, thank you for being here.

Mr. DANIELS. Thank you, Chairman. Thank you.

Chairman MCCAUL. I think it is fitting that this committee be the first committee to convene at the 9/11 Museum. This committee was formed in response to the tragic events of 9/11. This is a historic event, to have the Committee on Homeland Security have this hearing in this museum at this time this week.

I would like to thank the 9/11 Memorial and Museum for letting us hold the hearing today. I would also like to thank Mayor Giuliani and the other witnesses for taking the time to join us and for their service to this great city and to our country.

This morning, we are meeting on hallowed ground consecrated by the loss of thousands of innocent Americans and by the valor and sacrifice of those who worked to save their lives. In the wake of 9/11, we were told to never forget, and we did not. In their honor, we vowed, "Never again."

Our memories of the heroism we witnessed gave our Nation the resolve needed to embark on a generational struggle against Islamist terror. Fourteen years after that fateful day, we are still engaged in that struggle. But we have entered a new phase. The viral speed of violent extremism has allowed our enemies to spread globally and has brought the war back to our doorsteps. But we will not bow down to terror.

So we have come here today to draw on the lessons we learned after 9/11, to assess how we can make our country more secure, and to honor the memory of those we lost by rededicating ourselves to victory in this long war.

We have made progress since 9/11, which was the largest attack in world history. Our first responders are better-equipped, our intelligence professionals are connecting the dots, and our border authorities are keeping terrorists from stepping foot on our soil.

But our enemies have come a long way. Gone are the days of bin Laden, when extremists relied on couriers and caves to hatch their plots. Today's terrorists are openly recruiting on-line, across borders and at broadband speed. Radical groups like ISIS have enlisted citizens from over 100 countries to join their terrorist army in Syria. Islamist terror outposts have spread throughout the region and beyond. This includes Iran, the world's largest state sponsor of terror, which has extended its reach, and the results are alarming.

Last year was the deadliest year on record for global terrorism, and terrorists still have their sights set on the West. In fact, in the past 18 months, ISIS alone has inspired or directed nearly 60 plots or attacks against Western countries, including America. Authorities have also arrested an average of almost one American per week on terrorism charges.

We are in uncharted territory. Even at its height, al-Qaeda never reached this kind of operational tempo. Yet, in an age of peer-to-peer terrorism and cyber jihad, extremists can inspire new recruits on-line, tweet marching orders, and wait for fanatics to act. Their followers can also travel easily to join them overseas, where they are trained to wage war.

But, even though our adversaries evolved, the battle-tested principles we learned from 9/11 are still relevant.

First, we must remain vigilant. The 9/11 Commission found a Government-wide failure of imagination contributed to the surprise attack, so we must prepare for the worst and stay a step ahead of the threat.

We must also take the fight to the enemy before they can attack us here at home, and we can do this by eliminating terrorist sanctuaries overseas. Condoleezza Rice noted wisely, "If we learned anything from September 11, it is that we cannot wait while dangers gather." In 2004, the 9/11 Commission made the same point with an ominous prediction when they said, "If, for example, Iraq becomes a failed state," they wrote, "it will go to the top of the list of places that are breeding grounds for attacks against Americans at home. And if we are paying insufficient attention to Afghanistan, its countryside can once again offer refuge to al-Qaeda or its successor."

The lesson is clear: We must not let power vacuums develop in new places like Libya or in old safe havens like Afghanistan. Terrorists must be kept on the run, or else they will build larger armies and have the freedom to plot against us in relative safety.

September 11 also taught us that, in the long term, we must counter the ideology at the core of Islamist terror because, when left unchecked, it can spread to all corners of the globe in the same way communism and fascism led to decades of destruction.

I hope we will have a chance to examine these principles today and how to follow them in a new age of terror, but I also hope we can explore what the resolve of our 9/11 heroes can teach us about prevailing against those who seek to do America harm.

On that day, we saw the face of evil, as terrorists sought to attack our economic, military, and political centers of power, but we also saw the true heart of America, as ordinary men and women showed uncommon courage. First responders and pedestrians rushed into burning buildings and stormed cockpits to save one another. They were Americans with children, families, but they did not hesitate because they knew the people inside these buildings and with them on those airplanes had families too. Driven by common humanity, they knowingly put their lives in the hands of God. Their bravery has rightly earned them a certain measure of immortality.

He did not know it at the time, but when Todd Beamer said "let's roll" to his fellow passengers, he was leading them and us to the first victory in the war against Islamist terror. The day after, we were still reeling, but our Nation came together. We were Americans first. Even though we were uncertain about what the future held, we were united in our resilience to tragedy and in our resolve to deliver justice.

The column behind us here today is the final piece of debris removed from the World Trade Center site. Those who cleared the rubble inscribed it with the names, stories, and photos of people who perished, as well as the symbols of patriotism. So it is fitting that this last piece of the lower tower's wreckage now stands here as a permanent symbol of remembrance and resilience.

We are a country that did not invite aggression from dark corners of the globe, but, when it came to our shores, confidence and hope, not fear, rose from those ashes.

I want to thank everyone for being here today on this solemn occasion. I want to thank the witnesses.

[The statement of Chairman McCaul follows:]

STATEMENT OF CHAIRMAN MICHAEL T. MCCAUL

SEPTEMBER 8, 2015

This morning we are meeting on hallowed ground, consecrated by the loss of thousands of innocent Americans and by the valor and sacrifice of those who worked to save their lives. In the wake of 9/11, we were told to never forget them. We did not.

In their honor, we vowed "never again." Our memories of the heroism we witnessed gave our Nation the resolve needed to embark on a generational struggle against Islamist terror. Fourteen years after that fateful day, we are still engaged in that struggle, though we have entered a new phase. The viral spread of violent extremism has allowed our enemies to spread globally and has brought the war back to our doorsteps.

But we will not bow down to terror. So we have come here today to draw on the lessons we learned after 9/11, to assess how we can make our country more secure, and to honor the memory of those we lost by rededicating ourselves to victory in this long war.

We have made progress since 9/11, which was the largest terrorist attack in world history. Our first responders are better equipped. Our intelligence professionals are connecting the dots. Our border authorities are keeping terrorists from stepping foot on our soil. But our enemies have come a long way, too. Gone are the days of bin Laden, when extremists relied on couriers and caves to hatch their plots. Today's terrorists are openly recruiting on-line, across borders, and at broadband speed.

Radical groups like ISIS have enlisted citizens from over 100 countries to join their terrorist army in Syria, and Islamist terror outposts have spread throughout the region and beyond. This includes Iran, the world's largest state sponsor of terror, which has also extended its reach.

The results are alarming. Last year was the deadliest year on record for global terrorism. Terrorists still have their sights set on the West. In fact, in the past 18 months ISIS alone has inspired or directed nearly 60 plots or attacks against Western countries, including America. Authorities have also arrested, on average, almost one American a week on terrorism charges.

We are in unchartered territory. Even at its height, al-Qaeda never reached this kind of operational tempo. Yet in an age of peer-to-peer terrorism and cyber jihad, extremists can inspire new recruits on-line, tweet marching orders, and wait for fanatics to act. Their followers can also travel easily to join them overseas, where they are trained to wage war. But even though our adversaries evolved, the battle-tested principles we learned from 9/11 are still relevant.

First, we must remain vigilant. The 9/11 Commission found a Government-wide failure of imagination contributed to the surprise attack, so we must prepare for the worst and stay a step ahead of the threat. We must also take the fight to the enemy before they can attack us at home, and we can do this by eliminating terrorist sanctuaries overseas. Condoleezza Rice noted wisely: "If we learned anything from September 11, it is that we cannot wait while dangers gather."

In 2004, the 9/11 Commission made this same point with an ominous prediction: "If, for example, Iraq becomes a failed state," they wrote, "it will go to the top of the list of places that are breeding grounds for attacks against Americans at home. And, if we are paying insufficient attention to Afghanistan . . . its countryside could once again offer refuge to al-Qaeda, or its successor."

The lesson is clear: We must not let power vacuums develop in new places like Libya or in old safe havens like Afghanistan. Terrorists must be kept on the run or else they will build larger armies and have the freedom to plot against us in relative safety.

September 11 also taught us that in the long term we must counter the ideology at the core of Islamist terror, because when left unchecked, it can spread to all corners of the globe in the same way communism and fascism led to decades of destruction.

I hope we will have a chance to examine these principles today and how to follow them in a new age of terror. But I also hope we will explore what the resolve of our 9/11 heroes can teach us about prevailing against those who seek to do America harm.

On that day we saw the face of evil, as terrorists sought to attack our economic, military, and political centers of power. But we also saw the true heart of America, as ordinary men and women showed uncommon courage.

First responders and pedestrians rushed into burning buildings and stormed cockpits to save one another. These were Americans with children—with families. But they did not hesitate because they knew the people inside those buildings and with them on those airplanes had families, too.

Driven by common humanity, they knowingly put their lives in the hands of God. Their bravery has rightly earned them a certain measure of immortality. He did not know it at the time, but when Todd Beamer said "let's roll" to his fellow passengers, he was leading them—and us—to the first victory in the war against Islamist terror.

The day after, we were still reeling. But our Nation came together. We were Americans, and even though we were uncertain about what the future held, we were united in our resilience to tragedy and in our resolve to deliver justice.

The column behind us today is the final piece of debris removed from the World Trade Center site. Those who cleared the rubble inscribed it with names, stories, and photos of people who perished—as well as symbols of patriotism. It is fitting that this last piece of the tower's wreckage now stands here as a permanent symbol of remembrance and resilience.

We are a country that did not invite aggression from dark corners of the globe, but when it came to our shores, confidence and hope—not fear—rose from the ashes. Thank you.

Chairman McCAUL. The Chair now recognizes the Ranking Member.

Ms. SANCHEZ. Thank you, Mr. Chairman.

I want to thank New Yorkers, in particular, for allowing us to hold this hearing here.

Every time I come to this place, I am always overwhelmed, mostly because I had the opportunity to spend a lot of time in my earlier career here in the Twin Tower buildings. In fact, my former husband's office was here, and, because I was in the financial industry, we had plenty of friends at Cantor Fitzgerald. So, every time I come here, I remember all those innocent people who were taken on that day.

I want to thank our panelists for being here today.

I want to say that I am very proud of New Yorkers and Americans, because seeing this here today reminds me of just how resilient we are, how resilient—everything I know in the time that I have spent in this city—New Yorkers are. It is really a testament to our ability to never forget but to understand that the future is what we look forward to as Americans.

So, since 9/11, we have changed our policing and we changed the way that we engage our communities in order to prevent terrorist attacks. This committee has been on the forefront of trying to understand that and to help locals, in particular, because we know that you are the first responders.

I believe that law enforcement has become a great community facilitator, engaging in all facets of the city that they patrol. I see that they do it at a time, Mr. Chairman, when we are cutting back on the Federal funds that we send to the local jurisdictions. In fact, it has been a little alarming to me that the Congress has cut back on the funds.

For example, in 2011, Congress reduced the funding to only $1.9 billion to our local agencies. As a result of that, 32 cities were eliminated from the UASI program, for example. The following year, we appropriated only $1.35 billion to these important programs. Then we increased it a little bit; then we brought it back down again. Because of sequestration, we are looking again at cuts to our local law enforcement agencies for all the work that they have taken on ever, in particular, since 9/11.

I am also interested—I would like to hear from the locals about how that budget uncertainty, the amount of money that we put forward, does with respect to their programs and what you are really trying to do to ensure that a 9/11 or a Boston bombing doesn't happen.

Beyond dealing with that, I would like to hear about what you are doing with your local communities, including—for example, I represent the second-largest Arab-American community in our Nation, back in Orange County, California. I think that it is critical that we don't profile, that we don't unduly harass, and that we don't detain individuals simply because of how they look or what their religion is.

So I would like to hear from you, in particular, Commissioner Bratton, on how the New York Police Department engages communities such as Muslim Americans, especially after it was revealed that plain-clothes detectives went into Muslim neighborhoods to spy on that specific community, at least according to your *New York Times*. I understand that the NYPD dropped that program, but I would like to hear about how you are rebuilding that relationship and that trust with a community that we need to have on our side to help us with respect to local terrorism plots.

I look forward to hearing from both panels. I want to thank, again, the Chairman for holding the hearing.

I think that we have come a long way since 9/11 and that we still have a ways to go, but, again, I am always amazed at the resiliency of our people and at the resiliency of New Yorkers. I look forward to the testimony.

Thank you, and I yield back.

Chairman MCCAUL. I thank the Ranking Member.

Other Members are reminded opening statements may be submitted for the record.

[The statement of Ranking Member Thompson follows:]

STATEMENT OF RANKING MEMBER BENNIE G. THOMPSON

SEPTEMBER 8, 2015

I thank the Chairman for holding today's hearing.

Director Greenwald, thank you for hosting today's hearing at the National September 11 Memorial & Museum. The Museum serves a living tribute to those who lost their lives in the terrorist attacks and provides a daily education to future generations.

We are fortunate to have an exceptionally accomplished panel before the committee today.

Mayor Giuliani, I want thank you for joining us today and reflecting on your leadership during one of New York City's most difficult times.

Commissioner Nigro, you became chief of the Fire Department in the days following the 9/11 attacks. At that time, you led an organization that lost over 300 of its firefighters in the terrorist attack. I thank you for your service and look forward to hearing your testimony.

Commissioner Bratton, I also thank you for your service. Police officers are the boots on the ground that we need to prevent terrorist attacks. As the nature of the terrorist attack has evolved since 9/11, I look forward to hearing your perspective on this evolution.

Mr. Ielpi, we will never forget the over 3,000 people who lost their lives on September 11. Thank you for appearing today.

Mr. Thomas, during the September 11 attacks you were executive director of school safety for New York City Schools. As the person in charge of evacuation and coordination on that day, I want to hear the lessons learned and your insight on how coordination has improved since 9/11.

In the 14 years since September 11, America, particularly New York City, has shown its resilience and its resolve.

As we continue to honor those who perished aboard the hijacked planes on September 11 and those who sacrificed their lives trying to save others, we must not allow ourselves to be distracted by fear or guided by anger.

Rather, we must remain steadfast and determined in our efforts to thwart future attacks and ensure that our first responders have the training and support to do their jobs better and safer.

To do that, we cannot allow certain religious groups to be unjustifiably targeted by law enforcement and we cannot surrender the very civil liberties that make this country great. Instead, we must work hard to identify potential bad actors within the legal constructs of the Constitution.

Since 9/11, State and local law enforcement have been looked to as the first preventers in preventing terrorism.

The 9/11 Commissioners recommended that we stop stovepiping information and increase information sharing among Federal, State, and local authorities.

While increased information sharing is still necessary and gaps still exist, it has been proven that information sharing and coordination between the Federal, State, and local authorities have been helpful in preventing terrorist attacks.

In the 14 years since September 11, there have been at least 16 foiled terrorist plots targeted at New York City.

Some of these plots have been foiled by the cooperation between the Federal Bureau of Investigation, Joint Terrorism Task Force, and the New York City Police Department.

Increased police presence and sophisticated counterterrorism unit—which are funded in part by Federal dollars—have also been helpful in foiling terrorist plots in New York City.

Even though we recognize the importance of Federal funding to New York City and other jurisdictions, it is unfortunate that Congress continues to play chicken with the Federal appropriations process, which delays much-needed resources to State and local governments and first responders to build robust preparedness and response capabilities. This is unnecessary and should stop.

Instead, we should return to normal order so that States and first responder organizations can reliably plan for future training, exercises, and equipment investments.

We cannot become complacent in our support of first responders.

First responders have made significant progress in addressing challenges identified by the 9/11 Commission; maintaining and building upon that progress takes continued Federal support.

We cannot be complacent in fully implementing the recommendations of the 9/11 Commission.

To this day, Congress has still failed to consolidate jurisdiction of the Federal homeland security mission under one committee.

I hope that the Chairman will renew his effort to address this very important issue when we return to Washington this week.

I want to close by acknowledging and honoring those who died as a result of the September 11 attacks, or who are sick today because of their heroic actions 14 years ago.

Words cannot fully convey our sorrow for your loss or our gratitude for the sacrifices and bravery of so many first responders, but through action, we will try.

The James Zadroga 9/11 Health and Compensation Reauthorization Act would extend the authorization of programs critical to ensuring that first responders with 9/11-related illnesses get the care that they need and deserve and have access to compensation for associated economic losses.

We will work to ensure that this bill is enacted into law.
I yield back.

Chairman MCCAUL. We are pleased to have two distinguished panels of witnesses before us here today. The first: The former mayor of New York, Mayor Rudy Giuliani, will testify on the first panel. The second will consist of Mr. William Bratton, commissioner of the New York Police Department; and Mr. Daniel Nigro, the commissioner of the fire department for the city of New York; and Mr. Lee Ielpi, the president of the September 11th Families Association; and, finally, Mr. Gregory Thomas, president of the National Organization of Black Law Enforcement Executives and senior executive for law enforcement operations in the office of the Kings County District Attorney.

Let me first introduce the mayor.

If you would have a seat at the table.

Mayor Rudy Giuliani serves as a partner at Bracewell & Giuliani and is chairman and chief executive officer of Giuliani Partners. Previously, Mayor Giuliani served two terms as New York City's mayor, from 1994 to 2001, and led the city during and in the aftermath of the 9/11 attacks.

I can't think of a more important witness to be here today than you, sir. We thank you for your service both before but particularly after 9/11, where you brought—it was such a tragedy—brought this country together, sir. It is with great honor that we have you.

I now yield to you for your testimony.

STATEMENT OF HON. RUDOLPH GIULIANI, FORMER MAYOR, CITY OF NEW YORK, NEW YORK

Mr. GIULIANI. Mr. Chairman, it is a great honor for me to be here.

I thank the committee for holding the hearing here. As you said, there could be no more appropriate place. This is not just a museum; this is sacred ground. There are people buried here who were never recovered. So this is a very, very special place, not just to me but, I think, to everyone.

When I look at the wall behind you, I think of the days and weeks in which we worried that that wall wouldn't hold and this whole place would be flooded. We expended a great deal of time, energy, and money in trying to prevent that. Then, probably most of all, I think of all the caskets and people that were carried out here with American flags draped on them in great solemn procession.

I think of Father Judge, who was the first body that we found here on September 11, who was brought to St. Peter's Church, and remember his last words to me about 8 minutes before he died, which was, "God bless us." So maybe we should begin that way, with God blessing us.

This museum is many, many things. You will hear how one of the most important missions of this museum is so that people never forget. That is truly the case; they should not. Because we do have a tendency to repeat the mistakes of history. We have done that in the 20th Century several times, in de-arming after each war and then facing another war that we weren't prepared for. Hopefully, we won't make those mistakes again, and the reminder of what happened here will remind us of the fact that we face a very implacable and difficult foe.

The first point I would like to make is a point that I made very shortly after September 11, and that is that the Islamic terrorist war against us did not begin on September 11, 2001. I remind you, this very place was attacked in 1993, again by Islamic terrorists, who were taught their terrorism in a mosque in Union City, New Jersey, by an imam who is spending 100 years in jail now, sentenced by Judge Michael Mukasey, who eventually became Attorney General.

That wasn't the only mosque in New Jersey that was planning attacks on New York. It is unfortunately the case that there is an interpretation of the Islamic religion that calls for the destruction of our way of life. It is certainly not the majority view. It certainly doesn't reflect the views of most people of the Islamic religion.

On the evening of September 11, with the dust of September 11 on my jacket and in my eyes and on my face, I said to the people of New York that we should not view this as an attack by a particular group and assign group blame, that is the worst thing we could do, and that we should not attack anyone.

I sent, to the point made by Congresswoman Sanchez, I sent my police commissioner, Bernard Kerik, on the mission of tracking the number of attacks on members of the Arab community in New York. After 8 days, I stopped doing it because there were none. We expected it. We expected it because of the anger and the hatred. So, to the many things that New Yorker deserve credit, one of the things they deserve credit for is they don't engage in group blame.

But New Yorkers also aren't foolish, and we do realize that, although it isn't a matter of group blame, the word "profiling" has many meanings. If we are profiling based on objective evidence, that is exactly the way we investigate.

I was in law enforcement, as you were, for more of my life than anything else, and I caught criminals by profiling. When the victim told me the person was 6′4″, had blond hair and blue eyes, I didn't go look for a 5′4″ person with brown eyes and brown hair. If I did, I would have been a fool. I looked for a person that met the description of the people who committed the crime or might commit the crime.

The reality is that, whatever euphemisms we want to engage in, they are at war with us. By "they," I mean Islamic extremist terrorists. They kill in the name of Allah. They kill in the name of Mohammed. They interpret the Quran and the Hadith, which is the explication of the Quran—which, I might tell you, I have read several times—they interpret it and use those portions of the words of Mohammed that call for death to infidels. Unfortunately, they use mosques as breeding grounds for that—not all, but some.

Congresswoman Sanchez, I am the mayor who authorized the placement of New York City police officers in mosques in New Jersey and elsewhere, and Mayor Bloomberg continued it. I believe, by doing so, I saved the lives of many New Yorkers, because we uncovered plots that have never come to light. It is unfortunately the case that that has to be done. I believe it was a mistake to withdraw those patrols.

11

So, as we sit in a museum and when we go to museums, we think of history, don't we? If we were to go to Pearl Harbor and went to the museum in Pearl Harbor, we would think of history, the terrible attack on Pearl Harbor and the fact that that is now confined to history. Our enemies in those days are now our friends; they are some of our best friends—Germany, Italy, Japan. That war is over. We can go to Civil War memorials, and we can go to Revolutionary War memorials, some of which are in my great city, and that war is over. You are in a museum about a war that is still going on. Don't fool yourself into thinking that it is over.

Is it worse now or better now is a very debatable and maybe almost irrelevant issue, because it is very bad now. In certain areas, we have improved dramatically—airport security, airline security. Cooperation is considerably better between the Federal Government and local governments. All of that is true. But the threat remains, and the number of attacks in recent years have increased, and the number of threats have increased. The enemy has become considerably more diverse and, in that way, more difficult to track than when we were facing one major enemy, bin Laden.

But we made a mistake then, and I see us making the same mistake again if we are not careful. We made a mistake in not taking seriously what they were saying to us.

When they attacked us here in 1993 and killed our people under the orders of an imam from New Jersey, they had declared war on us. We treated it as a criminal act. It wasn't a criminal act like the 5,000 or 6,000 I prosecuted as United States attorney. It wasn't like the criminal acts of the mafia and Michael Milken and Ivan Boesky and corrupt politicians. It was an act of war.

Then, of course, they attacked us in East Africa or in Africa twice. Then they attacked our *USS Cole* and killed our servicemembers—by the way, an act of war, usually considered an act of war.

We largely ignored those attacks. Our response was tepid. Our response to the *USS Cole* was nonexistent. We allowed American servicemen to be slaughtered by bin Laden, and our reaction was nothing.

Just in case we weren't paying attention, bin Laden declared war on us. We weren't paying attention. Did that lead to September 11? Did that lead to a sense of arrogance, and did it lead to a sense of an America that was weak, an America that was unresponsive, an America that could be taken advantage of? No one will ever know. But it is safe to assume it did because it will protect us better in the future.

Then we had September 11. I lost numerous close personal friends, as did many of the people who are sitting here. It is extraordinarily difficult for me to return here. I have been to this museum only three times, and, the last time, I came with a group of Rangers who were going off on a mission, and their general wanted them to see where the war started that they are now having to continue.

But it didn't start here. It started way before here. The attack on the Munich Olympics was in 1972, on the Israeli team. The killing of Leon Klinghoffer was in the 1980s. We weren't listening, we weren't watching, we weren't paying attention, and we were taking peace dividends while people were declaring war on us.

I could trace the history of the aftermath of World War I and World War II and show you the same thing. Only fools repeat the mistakes of history. We are getting all the warnings again.

Yes, we have ISIS. ISIS has many causes, part of it the withdrawal of our troops from Iraq; part of it our unwillingness to engage in Syria; part of it the President drawing 12 red lines, saying that if Assad used chemical weapons he would act, and the President's red lines disappeared, which made America a hollow vessel, a Nation, one could assume, you could take advantage of. You don't draw red lines and then erase them and expect that implacable foes are not going to take advantage of that.

So we have ISIS doing things that take you back to the 6th Century and the 7th Century, to the acts of Ali and some of the followers of Mohammed—beheading of people, mass graves. Our response to ISIS so far has been, at best, to play defense; at worst, to be rather ineffective.

One of the great things that President Bush did for us, for which I said at the time will give him a place in history that can't be denied, is, after this attack took place, he immediately put this country on offense. By putting us on offense, he saved our city from repeated attacks.

There is no one, absolutely no one, who on the day of September 11, FBI or anyone else that briefed me, that didn't warn me that my city was going to be attacked numerous times in the future. Beginning with Commissioner Kerik, continuing through Commissioner Kelly and now Bratton, New York City has continuously grown its response to terrorism because we expect to be attacked again.

But we weren't attacked. We weren't, in large measure, because of the bravery of the men and women of our military, who went and engaged the enemy in Iraq and Afghanistan and kept them so busy that they couldn't plan attacks.

That presence of our military also brought us incalculable amounts of evidence and intelligence warning us about attacks. Consider how that is diminished when those troops aren't there. If you have 100,000 troops in a country, they are in villages, they are in towns, they talk to people, they gather intelligence. That intelligence gets to the CIA, it gets to the FBI, from the Joint Terrorism Task Force, it gets right down here to the streets of the city.

That is now gone. We do not have the benefit of that intelligence. It could be part of the reason we thought ISIS, or ISIL, was the JV, because we weren't getting the intelligence we were getting in the past. It is part of the reason we miscalculated them and let them catch up real fast. Now we are playing catch-up, not offense.

But ISIS is not the biggest threat to us. A determined, strong strategy of engaging our Special Forces could do a good job of eliminating ISIS. Our major threat—and let's not take our eye off it as we watch ISIS—is Iran.

The Iranian empire that began with the overthrow of the Shah and the first Ayatollah and now the second has killed well over a million people. We are talking about mass murderers. The Ayatollah and Prime Minister Rouhani have engaged in mass murder.

It is Prime Minister Rouhani who was the one who ordered the execution of the Jewish people in Argentina.

There are more people being killed in Iran today than under Ahmadinejad, for a very important reason: The Ayatollah and Rouhani do not want the people inside of Iran to drink the Koolaid of thinking that there is a reform going on in Iran. They are trying to get us to drink that Kool-aid. But they are killing people to remind their people, "We control Iran."

So let's not take our eye off Iran. Let's remember that we are negotiating with an Ayatollah who has pronounced the destruction of the state of Israel, the death of Americans, and has on his hands the blood of very, very many young Americans who were killed by the Quds Forces during the war in Iraq. We are negotiating with him.

At the same time we are negotiating with him and he is calling for our death and destruction, we are not calling for regime change in Iran. If they can have a two-part strategy in negotiating, why are we so unsophisticated that we can't have a two-part strategy? If the Ayatollah can negotiate with us and call for our death and destruction, then why can't we negotiate with him and call for regime change in Iran?

If Egypt needed regime change and we supported it and overthrew Mubarak, a friend of the United States and a friend of Israel; if we supported regime change in Iran and removed Qadhafi, who had been neutered—Qadhafi, a terrible man. I investigated Qadhafi, as United States attorney, for some of his acts, as I did Yasser Arafat, by the way, who was responsible for the murder of Leon Klinghoffer. If we could remove Qadhafi, who was useless as a threat, terrible to his own people but useless as a threat, if we could remove these people, why are we not for a regime change in Iran?

Iran has taken American hostages. Iran has killed thousands of Americans. Iran supports Hezbollah, Hamas, the Houthis in Yemen. Iran controls Iraq. We gave Iraq to Iran when we withdrew. Iran controls Syria through Assad.

Do you see what is developing? A Persian empire, a Shiite empire. To the south: Saudi Arabia, Jordan, the Emirates, Israel, Egypt. We have a very dangerous situation developing in the Middle East, where we have a divided Middle East. America is sitting back and not taking action to prevent it. Instead, it is negotiating an agreement that recognizes something that we have been fighting for decades, which is a nuclear Iran, which will make it even a bigger empire.

So I will conclude by saying that if this museum exists to remind us that we shouldn't forget and we shouldn't repeat the mistakes of history, let's let it do that. Let's realize that we are at war. If we don't want to call it that, they call it that. We have to respond in a way in which we are strong, assertive, intelligent.

This city has done everything it can to protect itself. The work of Commissioner Kelly, continued with the work of Commissioner Bratton, has been excellent.

It is absolutely necessary, as you pointed out during your opening statement, that we are now dealing with many diverse and smaller attacks, and it requires the FBI and the Federal authorities to think of our police as their eyes and ears. There are approximately 12,000 or 13,000 FBI agents; there are 35,000 New York City police officers. The New York Police Department is a much bigger law enforcement agency than the FBI. That is only one police department.

I could tell you attacks, when I was mayor before September 11, that were thwarted by intelligent New York City police officers who were trained to look for what Commissioner Bratton, I believe, originally termed as the "precursors of terrorism." We are going to need more of that, and this committee needs to encourage it.

It is hard to get agencies to work together; we all know that. But the work of this committee under you, Mr. Chairman, and under Mr. King has really been excellent in helping to bring those law enforcement agencies together. I urge that you continue to do that, because, although the threat may not be as large as it was with al-Qaeda, it is more diverse and harder to find, and the threat of Iran is greater than both.

Thank you.

Chairman MCCAUL. Thank you, Mayor, for those profound remarks. You are clearly the expert on this in the room.

I also want to commend the NYPD and the FBI and Homeland officials, who have worked well together—it didn't always used to be that way, as you know—to stop these threats. I have never seen these organizations working as well as they do today, which is evidenced by the amount of threats that we have stopped and the number of arrests that we have made, over 60 in the past year, to stop that. But they only have to be right once. People ask me what keeps me up at night. It is those cases that we don't know about.

You talked about 1979. It transformed the Middle East. We are still reeling from that today. We had flags, warning signs along the way. Ramzi Yousef, 1993 World Trade Center bomber, original targets: 12 Jewish synagogues, 12 tribes of Israel. Bojinka plot: 12 airliners, plotting with Khalid Sheik Mohammed, the mastermind of 9/11 that eventually came back to this target and unfortunately brought the Twin Towers down.

The job of this committee is to ensure that never happens again, but we have to see the warning signs along the way. There are many today.

I look at the uniform of the Navy Seal Team 6, the man who killed bin Laden, the Seal Team 6 who brought him down. But the threat didn't die that day with bin Laden. I think many have tried to downgrade that it is over, the war on terror is over.

I agree with you, sir. I was a Federal prosecutor like yourself. These are not criminal cases. This is a war that has to be clearly defined who the enemy is, and that is radical Islamists, extremists. Only through that can you defeat that enemy.

That was a great day, when bin Laden was killed, but it didn't end the threat. Now the threat is evolving. The threat is different. The challenge is different.

I believe this policy of containment against ISIS is not going to win the day, that as long as they can fester over there—after the Arab Spring, we have seen power vacuums fall, we have seen it filled by terrorists in Northern Africa and all throughout the Middle East. As that threat grows overseas over there, so, too, does the threat to the homeland, because they have greater territory to launch external operations, including operations over the internet that we have seen more recently.

So I guess my question to you, sir, is: There are many facets to this—militarily, politically, from an idealogical struggle. What more needs to be done to defeat this enemy?

Mr. GIULIANI. Well, I think I outlined some of it, which is I think there should be considerably more engagement in the parts of the world where people are plotting to kill us. It has always seemed to me it made sense to have American military in the places that were of most danger to us, which is the reason we kept our military in Germany for so long and in South Korea for so long.

I think the withdrawal of our troops from Iraq and Afghanistan on a time table will prove, historically, to be a horrible mistake. I believe it was the genesis of ISIS and our inability to properly assess ISIS.

I think the failure to have American troops in areas of great concern to us, meaning where people are plotting to kill us, deprives us of intelligence. Because it is the military that can gain a lot of that intelligence for us because of their interaction with people, informants and others that they come in contact with.

So I think there has to be an acknowledgment on the part of the administration that, whether we want to call it a war or not, it is a war, and the military should be engaged.

I also believe there should be more support for local policing, because this has come down to now trying to find the so-called lone wolf. Well, there have been so many lone wolves that it is a pack of wolves, not just a lone wolf. They are hard to find. They require training police officers in looking for, as I said before, the precursors of terrorism. It is a different kind of training; it is very specialized. It could use considerably more Federal support and help at the local level.

We can no longer rely just on the FBI, the CIA, the NSA, and even the military, because not all threats are coming from abroad. Some are. Some of the threats are coming from someone's home, and we need police officers who can observe suspicious activities.

We should not allow political correctness to override sensible law enforcement decisions about what needs to be done to protect lives. We shouldn't lose a single American life to political correctness.

Chairman MCCAUL. I think the foreign intelligence gained by the FBI and the intelligence community, combined with the street intelligence from our State and local police, working together, is the best way to protect the homeland from these threats.

My final question for you, sir, is: From your testimony, you appear to be opposed to the Iran negotiation, the Iran deal. Why do you oppose that agreement?

Mr. GIULIANI. I oppose that because I do not believe it makes sense to reach an agreement on the controlling of nuclear weapons with a mass murderer. I think history has proven that negotiations with mass murderers only lead to substantially more problems later.

I am extremely upset about the fact that the goals of that negotiation have changed. You might remember, the goal of the negotiation, including the U.N. sanctions originally, was for Iran to be non-nuclear. It now becomes, how nuclear should Iran be?

They should not have their hands on nuclear weapons. Iran does not need the peaceful use of nuclear power. It is not an energy-starved country. It is absurd to think that Iran needs the peaceful use of nuclear power. If we accept that, I would imagine the Ayatollah and his wise men are laughing at us, that we accept the idea that they need the peaceful use of nuclear power.

They are developing nuclear power for one reason and one reason alone: Because they want to create an empire, which we are letting them do. They control Iraq; we do not. They control Syria; we do not. They are basically at war with Saudi Arabia and Yemen through the Houthis. This is an enormously aggressive foe.

I learned a lesson from the Cold War. I had the great honor of working for President Ronald Reagan. President Reagan always had a nightmare, and that is why he ended the Cold War. But he ended the Cold War by pointing missiles at the Soviet Union and by telling them he would be willing to use those missiles. He ended the Cold War by developing, or beginning to develop, a nuclear shield that was laughed at and ridiculed. It is the nuclear shield that worked in Israel.

The reality is that we have to realize that we are putting the nuclear button in the hands of madmen. If the Ayatollah and the regime in Iran is not insane, it does a great pretense of being insane. To deny the Holocaust, to call for the destruction of one of our strongest allies, the state of Israel, to call for the death of Americans, to be responsible for American hostages for 444 days, and for killing thousands of Americans, I would have to say this is an insane regime.

Ronald Reagan's nightmare was mutually assured destruction was an immoral way to keep the peace, because if a madman got in control of the button in either place, the Soviet Union or the United States, the world could come to an end. Nuclear arms, nuclear capacity should not be put in the hands of madmen.

Chairman MCCAUL. Thank you, sir.

The Chair now recognizes the Ranking Member.

Ms. SANCHEZ. Thank you, Mr. Chairman.

Again, thank you, Mayor, for being before us. As usual, there are some things I agree with you on and there are some things where we differ.

Mr. GIULIANI. Sure.

Ms. SANCHEZ. Certainly, you and I have been on the same side with respect to Iran and its really terrible acts of violence that it does in inciting in particular in the Middle East and to its own people. So, on that, we definitely agree they are a terrible player.

But, you know, I have been 19 years in the Congress, 19 years on the military committee, No. 2 for the Democrats on the military committee now, 17 of those 19 years being on the subcommittee that does nuclear warfare, et cetera, doing Special Forces, I was the Chairwoman for Special Forces Subcommittee, et cetera.

I know that your expertise is not in the military. I really want to get to the area where I do believe you have extreme expertise in, and I want to elicit from you some information that we can use.

Mr. GIULIANI. Sure.

Ms. SANCHEZ. So I won't argue with you about what is going on with the military. I definitely have a different viewpoint. But I want to talk to you about the funding that the Federal Government—and the system in which we try to buttress what our local law enforcement are doing.

I mentioned in my opening statement that I am very concerned when I see Byrne or UASI or COPS grants or however it is that we are packaging from the Federal Government into our local law enforcement the funds and the fact that they are significantly decreasing over time, and, more importantly, the lack of predictability as to how those funds will flow, when they will flow, and for what they will flow.

Can you talk a little bit about, having overseen this city and, in particular, during the times of preparedness for your first responders, what that does to you and what you would see as more useful, from a funding perspective, from the Federal Government?

Mr. GIULIANI. Well, when I was the Mayor, I supported the crime bill. The crime bill was a great bargain between conservatives and liberals. It included social programs that a lot of conservatives disagreed with, and it included the death penalty and funding, tremendous funding, for local police that some liberals disagreed with.

Somehow, under President Clinton's leadership, he put together a group, bipartisan group, of mayors that included me and Ed Rendell, the Democratic mayor of Philadelphia, the Republican mayor of Los Angeles, and the Democratic mayor of St. Paul. From that, we received money for me to hire considerably more policemen. Commissioner Bratton and I received a great deal of funding. We were able to increase the size of our police department from, oh, I am going to say about 34,000, 35,000 to 41,000.

Aside from dealing with September 11, it helped us, certainly, in the massive reduction in crime, which, by the time I left, was a 65 percent reduction in homicide. But, on September 11, it left us with a large enough police department, although we did need help from other cities, that we were able to handle it and deal with it.

But, every year, the funding was in doubt. Every year, we had to make cutbacks and then restore. We tried to manage our way through it. I think we did. But you are absolutely correct; the funding should be—we should know what it is, and we should be able to plan on it for a 5- or 10-year period.

Law enforcement strategies—in particular, terrorism strategies—as the Chairman said, this is a long war. This requires 10 years of planning, 20 years of planning. Therefore, whatever funding Congress is going to provide, and the Federal Government, it should be consistent. As a mayor, which I no longer am, but if I was, or even, let's say, as a police commissioner or fire commissioner or head of emergency services, you should have a sense of what the funding is going to be 4 and 5 years from now.

The mayor of New York City is required to produce a budget for 4 years, which I think is very, very smart. I thought it was one of the great things that came out of the fiscal crisis of New York City. It removes a lot of one-shots and tricks. Because I have to show, if I reduce now, what is going to happen 4 years from now, or if I increase now—and we can't factor the Federal Government in.

I will make one final parochial point on behalf of my city. My city contributes considerably more to the Federal Government than the Federal Government contributes to the city. We are a donor city and a donor State, meaning we give you much more money in tax revenues than we get back in benefits. I am including all the benefits for Medicaid, Medicare, and the poor.

Senator Moynihan used to publish that report every year, and he and I would hold a press conference to show that New York City was being shortchanged by $7 billion or $8 billion, the State by about $12 billion.

So we don't come here as supplicants. We come here as contributors. We are giving you more money than you give us back. So at least give it back to us in a consistent way.

Ms. SANCHEZ. Mr. Mayor, thank you for that. I happen to represent Orange County, California, and we are also a donor county, believe me.

Mr. GIULIANI. I know you are, maybe by even more because you have become larger. My numbers are, like, 13, 14 years old.

Ms. SANCHEZ. So I understand and my people understand, in particular, the fact that we are community givers, in a sense, because we do pay more in taxes than we will ever receive back in that area.

Let me indulge, if you will, just one more question, Mr. Chairman.

This question is about, after the Boston Marathon bombings, the Harvard Kennedy School released a plan/action report where it identified the need for improved guidance regarding the role of political leaders and emergency managers during disaster response and how those entities ought to coordinate.

So, going back again to your mayorship—and the reason I ask you, not because I don't think you are doing important things today, but, you know, that was a very specific time where you had, really, the largest ever known disaster on our homeland. But I know, since then, you have been working with mayors in other cities to ensure that they are ready and that things are going well in case there should happen to be an attack that we don't stop in the planning stages.

So my question to you is: Can you describe your role in the incident command structure when you were here in New York, especially on that 9/11 day? What advice would you give other mayors and to us with respect to emergency managers and first responders during a disaster of that type? What lesson can we bring away from that, given your experience?

Mr. GIULIANI. Well, first of all, New York City is very fortunate in that it really isn't a city, it is a confederation of counties. We are five counties in the State of New York. In most cases, for example, in Miami or in Los Angeles, the city is an entity within a much larger county. Or let's take Boston. So when I had to deal with September 11 or the 30 or 40 other crises I had to deal with of a lesser scale—but since we have so many crises, our police, our firefighters, our emergency people are used to crisis. We have one entity.

In Boston, the report that you are dealing with is talking about having to coordinate 7, 8, 9, 10, 12, 15 different police departments, as many different fire departments, some of whom are volunteer fire departments, maybe an emergency services unit, maybe not.

So the job of coordination is much harder outside New York because New York is so big and because it is one entity. That doesn't mean we didn't have tremendous problems of coordination, but you can imagine that you multiply those problems by 10 or 20 when it is 7 or 8 or 9 different police departments that have to work together.

Governor Pataki and I made a decision shortly after the attack. It was, I would say, 40 minutes. I was trapped in a building for 20 minutes. When I got out, I called the Governor, and the Governor and I decided to put our governments together. We set up a headquarters, first at the police academy and then on the pier because the police academy turned out to be too small. We made all our decisions together. I would have a staff meeting every morning when I was mayor; he would, as Governor. We had our staff meeting together. We did that for 2½ months.

We did that because we realized that, first of all, a lot of bickering goes on between staffs that do not go on between principals. Second, there is a tremendous amount of bureaucracy in getting anything done, so if I had my commissioner and he had his commissioner and they were having a fight, we could resolve it right there and get it done and move it forward.

So my recommendation is you have to do exercises. I am a big believer in relentless preparation.

We had had numerous exercises in New York. At one point, we did an exercise with the Federal Government, pretending that there was a sarin gas attack right here at the World Trade Center. We brought in all the Federal and local people to see if they could work together, and we found out we knew very little about sarin gas and anthrax. Then we learned a lot about it.

We did a mock plane crash on the border of New York City and Nassau County to see how they would work together and to make sure they knew how to work together in case there was a plane crash at Kennedy Airport, which borders right on the beginnings of Nassau County.

We did table-top exercises like a possible sarin gas attack at a Knicks game, how would you evacuate?

So one of the things, among many, that I urge and probably the most important is: A tremendous amount of preparation. Go through the incident before it happens so that when it happens you are not going through it for the first time.

That is how I distinguish, let's say, the response to September 11, where the city, the State, and the Federal Government, which included FEMA, by the way, by that afternoon were sitting at the same table; and then the mistakes that were made in Katrina, where the Governor stayed in the capital and the mayor stayed in the city and FEMA stayed, well, somewhere.

Ms. SANCHEZ. The sheriff stayed on the bridge, as I recall.

Mr. GIULIANI. Yeah.

Ms. SANCHEZ. Thank you very much——

Mr. GIULIANI. Thank you.

Ms. SANCHEZ [continuing]. Mayor.

I am really blessed to represent an area where we have mutual assistance. So my 34 cities, the police and emergency and everything all fall under our sheriff——

Mr. GIULIANI. But they have to work at that.

Ms. SANCHEZ [continuing]. Then, under our sheriff, we fall under the L.A. sheriff if it should be larger.

You are right; I think one of the things we could do effectively, Mr. Chairman, is maybe to look at funding more of these exercises, because people really need to go through them to understand what to do when they happen.

Chairman MCCAUL. I know in Boston it helped out tremendously.

The Chair recognizes the gentleman from New York, Mr. King.

Mr. KING. Thank you, Mr. Chairman.

Rudy, it is great to have you here today.

I would just like to make a few points at the start.

One, I want to thank the Port Authority Police, the great job they do, and acknowledge my friend and neighbor, John Ryan, for the job he did as chief of the department.

Good to see you, John.

Also, I would like to just comment on a few things that have been said.

As far as the Homeland Security funding, we could always use more. There were some rough years, but I would say in the last several years it has stabilized. I actually commend Secretary Johnson for taking a number of those cities off the list, because the money should go to the cities that are targets. It makes no sense to be spreading Homeland Security funding all over the country. So this is a Democratic Secretary. I want to thank him for making the tough decisions and actually narrowing it down to the cities that really do need the money.

I have to say that New York's funding for the last 3 years has been consistent. When President Obama came in, he did try to cut the Secure the Cities program, but we worked with him, and that has now been stabilized.

So I would say that, while there are always problems and while we could always use more funding, the fact is that over the last several years New York has, I think, been treated fairly. I could ask, you know, Commissioner Bratton later, but I do think Department of Homeland Security has done a much better job on that.

As far as the issue of the NYPD, no one has done more to stop domestic terrorism in this country than the NYPD. I know *The New York Times* is quoted as saying that the NYPD spies. First of all, I would rely on *The New York Times* for absolutely nothing, and what they call spying I call good police surveillance. You don't have to believe me, but John Brennan, when he was President Obama's homeland security advisor, said the NYPD was the model for the entire country as far as combating Islamic terrorism.

If we are talking about profiling, whatever you want to term it, ethnic sensitivities, Rudy, you are Italian American, I am Irish American. When you were the U.S. attorney and you were going after the mafia, you went after the Italian American communities. I can tell you, when the FBI was going after the Westies, they hit every Irish bar in the west side of Manhattan. That is where they were, and that is where the arrests were made. Nobody was going to Harlem; nobody was going over there to find the Westies. They knew where to find them, and that was in the Irish neighborhoods.

So I think we should put political correctness aside. These are deadly enemies we face, and if we cave in to *The New York Times* and the Civil Liberties Union and these people who want to wring their hands—the fact is, under Mayor Bloomberg, under Commissioner Kelly, 16 plots against New York City in 12 years were stopped. Under Commissioner Bratton, in less than 2 years, there has been 12 plots, I believe, that were stopped.

What happened over the Fourth of July, what Bill Bratton did as far as stopping the threats against New York, the arrests that were made here in New York were just—again, if they had not been made, we would have a whole different climate here today. We came very, very close to being attacked over the Fourth of July by ISIS.

So I think that should be on the record and we should start talking realistically and not just talking metaphorically.

Rudy, you and I went to many funerals after 9/11, too many. We saw all the cops—the cops were killed, the firefighters were killed, Port Authority cops were killed. But people are still dying. Cops and firefighters are still dying as a result of the illnesses they incurred. I think the fire department alone—and Commissioner Nigro can talk with more authority on this—they have lost—I think 111 firefighters have died since 9/11 from 9/11-related health illnesses.

So I would ask you, again, as the former mayor who did a phenomenal job—and we can never thank you for the leadership you showed on September 11 and those weeks afterwards where you basically held the entire country together—the importance, if you could just speak, of extending the Zadroga Act. It expires this year; the funding will end next year. There are thousands and thousands of people from all over the country, firefighters, cops, who came to New York to volunteer. I think 429 Congressional districts have people. The importance of that being extended and the suffering that those people are going through.

Mr. GIULIANI. Well, first of all, it is of critical importance. It shouldn't even be a question. It is a matter of duty that we owe to these people.

I can tell you, as the mayor at the time and going through the trauma and shock of September 11, to have people come here from all over the country to help us was enormously important, for two reasons.

First of all, even though New York City has the largest police department, the largest fire department, the largest emergency services components, significant presence of FBI and everything else, this attack was beyond our capacity.

When I talked to Governor Pataki on the phone shortly after getting out of the building I was trapped in, the Governor thought I had died, and he said, "Thank God. We thought you were lost." He said, "Mayor, I know you don't like this, but I have prepositioned the National Guard, and I have put them on Randalls Island."

Now, why he said that was I always resisted the National Guard in New York City for any kind of civil disturbance, because, No. 1,

I was quite confident my police department can handle it, and, No. 2, I don't like putting the National Guard in a law enforcement situation because there are differences that they are not trained for, and I don't want to see them getting in trouble doing something that a cop would know you can't do.

When he said that, I had a totally different reaction, though. I said, "Thank you for getting the National Guard, and if you can get 10 more of them, I need them." September 11 was way beyond New York City, so I needed all the help that I could get.

Mayor Daley from Chicago sent me police officers and firefighters. Governor Bush from Florida sent me State police officers. I got help from Maryland, I got help from Indiana, I got help from every part of the country.

No. 1, we needed the help. No. 2, we needed the emotional support even more than the help. We needed the feeling that we weren't alone, that we were being supported by the rest of the country.

Think of it as the loss of a loved one. Your first feeling is that you are all alone, and then you have a wake or a gathering, and people come and hug you and squeeze you, and now you realize you are not alone in your trauma. Well, the presence of all those people that came here was enormously important.

Many of them sacrificed their health to do that. I knew from the moment that started that this would be an enormously dangerous operation and was very worried that people would die. Almost saw a firefighter have his head decapitated by a crane that swung around, and he was tackled by another firefighter, who saved his life.

So, look, these illnesses we don't understand. The simple fact is it has never happened to us before, so, at the time that it was happening and to this day, we are doing the best we can to try to figure out what the damage is, physical and psychological.

I know people that are suffering from PTSD as a result of September 11. It is horrible to see, but they are. That is not going to stop tomorrow. That is going to go on next year and the year after and the year after.

So I think this should be continued if we really mean that we are not going to forget.

Mr. KING. Thank you, Rudy. Thank you for your service.

Chairman MCCAUL. The Chair recognizes Ms. Jackson Lee.

Ms. JACKSON LEE. Mr. Chairman, thank you so very much. Let me thank both you and our Ranking Member, Bennie Thompson, for your leadership.

I think it should be noted here in New York, Mayor, that this is one of the most bipartisan committees in the United States Congress, and I am grateful for it. Because I certainly was not you, but, as a Member of Congress, I sought to come to this sacred place as soon as I could, and, in actuality, I managed to arrive when there was still the recovery process going on and became one of the early Members of the Homeland Security Committee, and, ultimately, the Department was created.

We thank you for your service. We thank those—I had my office just print out for me the names of firefighters, police officers, fire marshal, and the chaplain you mentioned, just to reinforce for America that these souls gave their life for this Nation.

As I walked into this place, I could not help but read, "No day shall erase you from the memory of time." I think, as Members of Congress, this is something that maybe we should carry for all of our very weighty decisions that we will be making.

I know you know that we will be discussing a very important agreement come this week. I will not choose to discuss the Iranian non-nuclear agreement, but what I will say to the American people and to those that are listening, this will be a very vigorous debate with Members of Congress seriously considering the security of this Nation. Some of us will vote "yes" because we have deliberated and believe it is the right decision. But what I want to give you comfort is that it will be a very vigorous, thoughtful discussion, working on behalf of the American people, as you have done.

So I want to proceed to talk about the people whose lives were lost and whose memories will never be erased. To join with my colleague—and let me, of course, acknowledge Congressman King and Kathleen Rice and John Katko, New Yorkers, who have been outstanding on this committee. I thank them for their service and others who have gone on.

But let me again agree with Congressman King. I am a champion of the reauthorization of this legislation dealing with those who were impacted. So I just want to be somewhat redundant and ask the question, is it not imperative that we as quickly as possible reauthorize the James Zadroga legislation, primarily because of what you said, but is there urgency there? Because, as I understand it, there are individuals whose sicknesses are being discovered, the length of sicknesses, people who are losing their lives. Is it imperative that we sort of move quickly on this?

Mr. GIULIANI. The simple answer is yes, and I underline that. It is important that you do move on it.

I also would like to acknowledge, Congresswoman, from our previous encounters in the past that I know the bipartisan nature of this committee, how it has always worked to do the very best that it could to try to improve homeland security. I must tell you, just as someone who works in the field of security, I greatly appreciate what you do on both sides of the aisle and try very, very hard to reconcile differences, because you realize, as we did immediately after September 11, that, in protecting ourselves against terrorism, we are not Democrats and Republicans, we are Americans.

Ms. JACKSON LEE. I have another, sort-of, directed question, if I could. We have heard different perspectives on the funding, but I want to ask the question, the value of consistent funding for police departments, first responders having an ability to plan. You noted that you have a 4-year budget here, and, therefore, you would be willing to do that.

As I do that, I can't leave out my city of Houston. Everyone has mentioned their area, and I want to bring greetings from the former mayor of the city of Houston, Mayor Lee P. Brown, who was a commissioner here in New York that many of you know and served very ably, and to note that Houston was one of the cities rumored on that day, primarily because of the energy resources that were there.

But the consistency of funding, how important is that?

Mr. GIULIANI. It is very important. You know, it is like in business. Most people in business will tell you what we need to know is what we are going to get or not get and then we can make plans.

Since the budget in New York City is an enormously complex process—it is now, I believe, a $78 billion budget, almost double the size it was when I was mayor—consistency is enormously important, in other words, knowing what you can count on so then you can go figure out how to make up the difference somewhere else.

Ms. JACKSON LEE. One last quick question, Mr. Chairman, if I could.

I would like to submit into the record, Mr. Chairman—and I am going to combine a question to the mayor—H.R. 2795.

Mr. Mayor, it is a bill that I have introduced called the FRIENDS Act, which is to assess the impact on first responders of the concerns regarding their families when they are being called off and may spend long days and hours away, the responsibility of the Homeland Security Department to look into resources for the families of first responders while they are engaged in fighting the war on terror, on the incident or the impact of war on terror.

I would like to submit this into the record, H.R. 2795.

Chairman MCCAUL. Without objection, so ordered.

[The bill follows:]

H.R. 2795

114th CONGRESS · 1st Session

To require the Secretary of Homeland Security to submit a study on the circumstances which may impact the effectiveness and availability of first responders before, during, or after a terrorist threat or event.

June 16, 2015

Ms. JACKSON LEE (for herself, Mr. PAYNE, Ms. FUDGE, Ms. KELLY of Illinois, Mrs. BEATTY, Mr. PASCRELL, Ms. DELAURO, Mr. LARSON of Connecticut, Mr. NORCROSS, Mr. CASTRO of Texas, Mr. GENE GREEN of Texas, Ms. BASS, Ms. LEE, Mr. HINOJOSA, and Mr. PALLONE) introduced the following bill; which was referred to the Committee on Homeland Security

A BILL

To require the Secretary of Homeland Security to submit a study on the circumstances which may impact the effectiveness and availability of first responders before, during, or after a terrorist threat or event.

Be it enacted by the Senate and House of Representatives of the United States of America in Congress assembled,

SECTION 1. SHORT TITLE.

This Act may be cited as the 'First Responder Identification of Emergency Needs in Disaster Situations' or the 'FRIENDS Act'.

SEC. 2. CIRCUMSTANCES WHICH MAY IMPACT FIRST RESPONDERS DURING A TERRORIST EVENT.

Not later than 260 days after the date of the enactment of this Act, the Secretary of Homeland Security shall submit to the Committee on Homeland Security of the House of Representatives and the Committee on Homeland Security and Governmental Affairs of the Senate a report on factors that would result in first responders failing to meet expectations based upon training and planning for terrorist incidents. The report——

(1) may include information on first responder performance and availability before, during, or after a terrorist threat or event; and

(2) shall——

(A) include first responder input on how the presence of family in the impacted area, the adequacy of personal protective equipment, and training gaps may influence performance and availability; and

(B) contain recommendations to the Committee on Homeland Security of the House of Representatives and the Committee on Homeland Security and Governmental Affairs of the Senate.

Ms. JACKSON LEE. Thank you.

Mr. Mayor, then let me follow up my question on that. As I said, this bill deals with the idea of not leaving these first responders burdened with, "What is happening to my family?", that we should have some sort of response plan for families left behind while they are on. So I am going to ask you whether that is a valuable thinking that we should engage in.

But I want to raise this point. As I started out, I indicated that this place, this hallowed ground was very moving to me as I walked in. I wanted to take a moment to honor the thousands of victims on this hallowed ground and those in Shanksville, Pennsylvania, and the Pentagon, which those of us who were in Congress at that time, Mr. Mayor, actually were there and saw as the plane came down on the Pentagon—it is a very real vision in our minds and our psyche—and to acknowledge those military personnel, as well, who went forward into battle after this time.

As I note this particular hearing title, it does sort-of throw us into the arms of fear somewhat. I want to end on celebrating the bravery and the sacrifice of those who lost their lives. I would like to—because you have said that, any moment, we are subjected to the possibility of a terrorist act anywhere in the United States where the bad guys think that they can make a statement to the world about our democracy and our peace.

So I would like you first to comment on the value of trying to think about the families of first responders. Then, second, I would like you to think about what I think you are proud of, is that New York City is a hallmark of resiliency and how it rebuilt itself from devastation and, in that, how we should be—I guess I am asking three questions—how we should be concerned about home-grown terrorism with the attitude that we stigmatize no race, no group, but we are conscious about that potential.

So the FRIENDS Act, which is about the families; the resiliency; and then home-grown terrorists.

Mr. GIULIANI. Well, the FRIENDS Act makes a great deal of sense, Congresswoman. The reality is that the families suffer sometimes more than the responders. I have found, not just on September 11 but with the loss of almost 50 firefighters and police officers before September 11——

Ms. JACKSON LEE. Yes.

Mr. GIULIANI [continuing]. That the men and women who were engaged in the activity have the adrenaline and the, sort-of, satisfaction of doing what it is they believe they can do best. It is the families that are left behind to suffer.

I come from a family with four uncles who were police officers and one who was a firefighter. He had been seriously injured twice, and I know how devastating that was on my family. When you get a big incident like this, this is something where there should be support for the families.

I am very glad you mentioned the word "resiliency," because I am enormously proud of the following fact: There are twice as many people that live in this area of New York today than before September 11.

On September 11 and in the days after September 11, we weren't sure anybody was going to return here. The people who lived here had to be moved out; the businesses had to be moved out. Thank goodness to two companies, Merrill Lynch and American Express, who made clear immediately they would return. Other companies, I would have to spend enormous amounts of time on the telephone and in person begging them, pleading with them to come back. This went on for some time. I don't think we ever thought we would be able to get it back even to where it was.

But to demonstrate the resiliency of New Yorkers and Americans, there are twice as many people living here today than before September 11. They fully recognize that this is a target, but they also realize that you have to have life go on and you can't let these terrorists terrorize us, right?

Ms. JACKSON LEE. Absolutely.

Mr. GIULIANI. A defense to terrorism is resiliency.

Ms. JACKSON LEE. Absolutely.

Mr. GIULIANI. It is a more subtle defense but a very, very important one. The resiliency of New Yorkers has been, I think, a real model, for which the people who live here should get great, great credit.

This is a very vital community. It has Little Leagues, it has soccer leagues. This has become a community. Twenty years ago, this was purely, as you know, offices. This was Wall Street. Wall Street moved to Midtown, really, and this has become a mixed business/residential community. It is one of our most vital. Unfortunately, it is starting to get too darn expensive for a lot of people, but that is what happens.

The second thing is, thank you for mentioning the bravery of the firefighters and police officers.

The September 11 Commission, when they concluded with their recommendations and conclusions, made some very helpful observations—some laudatory, some critical, all very helpful. But one of the things they pointed out was that the New York City Fire Department saved 98 percent of the people they were capable of saving.

I would like this committee to know that the first estimate that I was given of the number of losses was 12,000. That was the first number. By the end of that day, when I was asked the question, "How many casualties do you think you had?", the number that I had from all of our sources was 6,000. That is why I said—I didn't mention a number, and I said, it is just too much for us to bear to talk about that right now.

Turned out to be less than 3,000. That is a terrible number, and it is the worst domestic attack in our history.

Ms. JACKSON LEE. Yeah.

Mr. GIULIANI. But the reason it wasn't 12,000 or 6,000 is because the firefighters and the police officers stood their ground, even when they were given an evacuation order. An evacuation order to a New York City firefighter means—or police officer—"I leave when all the civilians are gone," which means they were the last ones to leave, which is why so many of them died.

But I can't tell you how many people come up to me, including outside the United States, who were in this building that day and thank me. You know what they say to me? Thank you for your firefighters, because if they hadn't remained calm, we could have lost more people in the evacuation than we lost in the attack. Now, I am not sure that is true, but they believe that.

But we know of many evacuations that are chaotic and that lead to death during the evacuation. This was not a chaotic evacuation. This was an orderly, very well-handled evacuation. It only was that because these men and women gave up their lives. That is a source of, I think, tremendous strength for America.

Imagine if the headline the next day, in addition to the fact that this was the worst attack in our history, was: It also was characterized by firefighters and police officers who ran away. Can you imagine how that would have affected the morale of the United States? How different was it that the headline the next day was about a terrible attack but also stories of incredible bravery on the part of the fire department, the Port Authority, the police department, and also single individuals, like from Morgan Stanley and others, who played the same role.

Ms. JACKSON LEE. Thank you very much. We are not allowing terrorists to terrorize us.

Mr. GIULIANI. That is absolutely right.

Ms. JACKSON LEE. Thank you.

I yield back.

Chairman McCAUL. I thank the gentlelady.

We have 8 members left for questions. We have a second panel. I am going to have to strictly enforce the 5-minute rule.

With that, I recognize Mrs. Miller.

Mrs. MILLER. Thank you. I appreciate you enforcing the 5-minute rule.

Mr. Mayor—and I say that with the highest degree of respect, because, sitting here today in this place, in this sacred place, and having the opportunity—it was my first time to be here last night, and Joe gave us a tour of this facility. Every American thinking about where they were on that day. I think we were all talking about, where were you, where were you, what happened, what your thoughts were, et cetera.

But when we think about—one of the things I think about then is that you, not being just the mayor of New York City, you were America's mayor at that time. You became America's mayor. The entire world looked to you for your news conferences so we could figure out what was happening. We would say, oh, well, here is Rudy, he will tell us what is going on. We were listening to you all the time.

So being here today in this place and listening to you and your thoughts and remembrances are certainly a bit overwhelming, as some other Members have said, certainly emotional.

But I think I am going to go right to picking up a little bit what you just talked about, the 9/11 Commission and some of the recommendations they made. Because, really, one of the things that— as you said, it didn't start on 9/11, but I think many people realize that we are facing such a different enemy than our country has ever faced before.

The battlefield has changed. You don't see now over on this hill where everyone has got the same kind of uniform where you can immediately identify them. No, we are facing cockroaches, cowards. It is an asymmetrical battlefield, in urban settings now.

Who responds? Not the military, in many cases, right? It is the first responders that are responding all over the country when there are things, whether it just happened in Chattanooga, various things that have happened here.

But one of the key recommendations, I think, that came out of the 9/11 Commission was they said there were so many of the different agencies that were stovepiping their ability to communicate to one another. Really, the inability to communicate. I think, certainly, I have heard you speak on many occasions about some of the handicaps that you had here and the inability to communicate properly with one another.

The 9/11 Commission said we need to go from the need to know to the need to share, the need to share information from all various agencies. Yet we still learned some of the lessons—you mentioned about the Boston Marathon bombings there, where, really—and we had a hearing on this. You know, you have 12,000, 13,000 FBI agents across the country; as you mentioned, there are 35,000 police officers here in New York City alone.

One thing about the street, the street talks. The street talks. The ability to have law enforcement gather the information, share the information, and, from our best intelligence in our country, to make sure it gets down to the boots on the ground, and having interoperability, et cetera.

So I guess I would just like to have you expand a little bit on how important it is to have the interoperability, the ability to communicate, the most simple thing in human behavior, communication, and how important it is, and for the Federal Government's role in making sure that we get the resources out into the first responders, that people can talk to one another about what is coming, what is happening, God forbid, when there is some other attempt, attack, what have you.

Mr. GIULIANI. Well, I will be very brief, because I think Commissioner Bratton can give you more details on this, because, both here and in Los Angeles, he was in the forefront of developing criteria that you use to try to identify terrorists. Well, it is all well and good to have that criteria or precursors of terrorism, and the New York City Police Department utilizes it, but I am not sure that is being done all over the country.

It needs to be done, because, as we have now found out, although New York is a big target and the main target, I think we are now turning into a situation where there are many targets. With these lone wolves or smaller groups of terrorists, I think we are going to see smaller towns and more isolated places attacked. In a way, that produces its own kind of fear, like you are not safe anywhere.

Therefore, this committee, I think, could play a very useful role in helping the Department of Homeland Security in I think what one of its main missions is, which is to make sure that every police department, every fire department, every emergency services department in the United States has at least a basic ability to deal with spotting terrorists, identifying terrorists, and then how to react if it happens.

I very much appreciate your description of them as cockroaches, because that is a great example of the difference. These people are emerging from the ground. It is the police officers that patrol the streets who have the most knowledge of the ground. Sometimes it is the police officers who can interpret the intelligence better.

There was one incident during September 11 when it took me 4 hours to get the information from the Federal Government that I needed for my police commissioner and police department to interpret. I wanted the words. They had increased the threat on New York, but they wouldn't give us the words that were used. I finally was able to impress on—well, I won't say who in Washington. I think I said something like, "I might cancel the World Series," because I wanted the words.

Now, why did I want the words? I wanted the words because, if I could share that with my police department, the words, which may mean nothing to an analyst in Washington, might give a hint to my police officers that it is a bridge, a tunnel, a building that is going to be hit, because they may understand something in the language because they know the city. The analyst in Washington doesn't know the city, but our cops on the street know the city.

One of the excuses I was given was, we don't share information like this with local law enforcement because local law enforcement leaks, to which, even though it was shortly after September 11, I just laughed and said, "You are talking to somebody who was a Federal prosecutor for 17 years, and don't tell me the FBI doesn't leak. Ha."

So my department doesn't leak any more than the FBI, and we are not going to leak this information, because we know how critical it is. We don't have time to worry about leaks because, if you give it to me now, it can be actionable information. Otherwise, I am going to read about it 4 days later in *The New York Times* anyway. So you might as well give it to me.

Your committee can perform a very useful function in breaking down that barrier. The protection against these cockroaches are our local police, but they need to get information in order to know what to look for. It is not just give information; they need to get information.

These joint terrorism task forces are quite an effective way to do that, and I would really consider expanding them.

Mrs. MILLER. Thank you, Mr. Mayor.

Thank you, Mr. Chairman.

Chairman MCCAUL. The World Series went forward, and the President threw a perfect strike, as I recall, right?

Mr. GIULIANI. As challenged by Derek Jeter.

Chairman MCCAUL. The Chair recognizes Mr. Vela.

Mr. VELA. Thank you, Mr. Chairman. Thank you for holding this hearing in these solemn grounds. I think, as we go back to Washington, it is important to go back there with the perspective of knowing that what happened here was such a tragedy and that we owe it to our country to honor those who fell and who lost their lives.

Thank you for your compelling testimony, Mayor. Thank you for reminding us how this area has flourished since 9/11.

On 9/11, I was under a court order to take a deposition in New York City about a week later. You can't live too much further away, if you are an American, than I do, because I am from Brownsville, Texas. Opposing counsel and I had to make a decision, because there weren't too many flights going out, so we decided to drive. It took us 3 days. I remember, when I got here, it wasn't the New York City that I was used to visiting. I remember how quiet it was. I remember the dust. I remember just how gray it was.

Then, several years later, I stayed at the very hotel across the street that we stayed in last night. I remember thinking to myself, I will never stay here again, because, by that time, the jack-hammers had come back and they were starting to rebuild.

Then, last year, at the invitation of Congressman Crowley, my friend from Queens, I had the pleasure of touring the new Freedom Tower. I was on the 64th floor, and the Port Authority gave us a tour. I remember being on that top floor and thinking to myself what a great tribute it was to the people of this city to be rebuilding.

Then, of course, here we are today.

But, at the end of the day, the most important thing about this hearing is that we, the American people, owe the people of New York a great deal of gratitude for rebuilding and for honoring the people that died here that day.

I am going to limit my questions. I have two questions, and I am going to limit them to this.

That is, we talked about the diversity of the threat that we face today, because it is not just in New York, it is all over this country. I am curious about what your assessment is. We know how prepared the city of New York, through Federal, State, and local cooperation, is to deal and prevent these threats—16 in the last several years. What is your assessment of how other places around the country are prepared to prevent those threats?

Mr. GIULIANI. Well, first of all, Mr. Vela, may I say that September 11 brought us together much closer than a country has ever been for about 2 or 3 months—no Democrats, no Republicans, no liberals, no conservatives, just Americans working together. But I can tell you, in New York, opposing counsel would never be able to drive in the same car to Brownsville, Texas, without beating the heck out of each other.

Mr. VELA. Well, we did drive separately.

Mr. GIULIANI. Oh, okay. Now I got it. Okay. Because I know lawyers—lawyers aren't affected by any of this.

But may I just interrupt for one second to suggest to you that one of the funding things you should consider is funding this as a National museum. There is a bill pending to do that. This really should be a National museum, because it affected the whole Nation. I would just like you to know how important I believe that is, that this be funded as a National museum.

Mr. VELA. We will take that back to our committees of interest.

Mr. GIULIANI. I am sorry, the rest of the question?

Mr. VELA. Yeah, I was curious what your assessment is of how other communities are——

Mr. GIULIANI. Oh, yes. It is very mixed, to be honest. In my ability to get around and talk to the police—and I travel a great deal. Some cities and counties are tremendously well-prepared, and some are not well-prepared.

I have always thought that the mission of the Department of Homeland Security is to get every place in America ready and to sort-of set a standard that every community should reach. I mean, everyone should understand anthrax and sarin gas and biochemical or biological agents and how to detect them. That is a function that the Department of Homeland Security should monitor.

The present head of the Department of Homeland Security was one of my assistant U.S. attorneys, and I have great respect for him, and I think he is doing a very good job of trying to do that. Any assistance you can give him in that regard, I think, would be enormously important.

I think we have to think of the fact that, although New York is a major target, as is the District of Columbia or Los Angeles, these new terrorists—let's call them that—might be thinking, let's attack them in places of less resistance, let's look for——

Mr. VELA. Like Chattanooga.

Mr. GIULIANI. Like Chattanooga. Therefore, what that means is a tremendous burden on the Secretary of Homeland Security and the Homeland Security Department to get a lot of departments that wouldn't necessarily face a lot of emergencies up to speed.

I think your encouragement and sensible funding of that, working with Jeh Johnson, could be a very important thing, because it is something he understands and it is something he is trying to do.

Mr. VELA. Thank you.

Chairman MCCAUL. Mr. Katko is recognized.

Mr. KATKO. Thank you, Mr. Chairman.

Mayor, on 9/11, I remember standing in the U.S. attorney's office in Syracuse, where I was an organized crime prosecutor, and watching the events unfold, and it left an indelible impression on me. But what also left on impression on me was your leadership that day and your leadership in the days and months thereafter. I think you had a profoundly positive effect on our country, and I thank you for that.

Since that time, I have watched you gain more experience and more knowledge on the whole terrorist threat globally and with respect to the United States. As I see it, the threat matrix has changed. Back on 9/11, people came to this country to attack us. Now we have the phenomena with ISIS where people within this country of ours, American citizens, are being implored to take up arms against the country, go blow up something, go shoot something.

It is a very different threat matrix now, and I would very much like to have your impression on what you think is the best way to attack it.

You kind-of touched on it with respect to the violent extremism and how it is branching out to different areas, it is not necessarily centered in one city right now or New York City, for example.

The biggest thing that I am concerned about now is, how do you counter that violent extremism in the communities? One of the things I think we need to focus on is, in those communities Nationwide, when we see people who might become radicalized, what do you do? How do you go about fighting it? How do you go about interceding before somebody who is drifting in the wrong direction does something terrible?

I would like to hear your input on that.

Mr. GIULIANI. Well, first of all, the idea that there would be lone-wolf attacks or attacks that were self-generated, 2, 3 people who were natives of the country doing this, in a way, our government, starting about a year ago, was acting as if this was a big surprise.

Bin Laden wrote about this in 1997, and some of his surrogates encouraged this in 1998 and 1999. Gosh, it happened in London in 2005; those were home-grown terrorists. I don't know why we are so far behind all the time. It is——

Mr. KATKO. Again, we are not heeding the warnings.

Mr. GIULIANI. Yeah. I mean, I was one block away from the first bomb that went off in the Liverpool station with exactly the same police officer who was with me and got me out of the building I was trapped in—which was a heck of a coincidence, and it stopped getting me invited anywhere for about 5 years. But, if I recall correctly, all four of those bombers were citizens of the United Kingdom and two of them were born there.

So, I don't know, I would think we would have started then saying to ourselves, this is a threat. Well, okay, finally, in the last year, we have recognized it.

It does require a different law enforcement strategy, and it requires a different military strategy. It requires, as I said, the use of the police in a much more energetic way and a much more informed way as our eyes and ears.

It also requires something that is controversial, but it is true: It requires understanding there is an organizing principle. These are not singular acts of crime like, you know, the shooting that took place in Brooklyn the other night at the West Indian parade or a shooting that might take place in Chicago or a shooting that might take place here or there, whatever.

There is an organizing principle, much like the mafia was an organizing principle. A mafia murder in New York was different than a murder in New York. The mafia murder in New York had an organizing principle behind it, and these attacks have an organizing principle behind it. It is called their interpretation of how Mohammad taught jihad, on which Islamic scholars could have great debates.

One interpretation of jihad is to remove or subjugate the infidel. This comes out of Islamic literature. Many reformed Muslims reject it, but some Muslims accept it.

So there is an organizing principle here. If we act in a state of denial out of political correctness that this is the organizing principle, then we are going to miss a lot of these situations. Because that helps to give us some of the criteria that we are looking for that some people think, you know, should be ignored.

So the reality is we need to train our police, we need to realize that the organizing principle here is jihad and their interpretation of it. That means we look in the places where that is going to be taught and exploited—social media, unfortunately mosques, certain groups that are more extremist than others—and that we somehow say the words "Islamic extremist terrorist" and not be condemned as bigots for saying it.

Congressman King made a reference to the mafia. When I indicted the first group of mafia members in New York and referred to them as "the mafia," I had a demonstration in front of my office by the Italian American Civil Rights League.

The Italian American Civil Rights League was founded by a man named Joe Colombo, who was the head of the Colombo crime family.

I also found out something I didn't know. In the Justice Department manual, it was improper to refer to a group as "the mafia." I could have been penalized. You know they love to penalize in the Justice Department.

Mr. KATKO. Oh, yes. I was there for 20 years.

Mr. GIULIANI. Yeah.

Mr. KATKO. I understand that.

Mr. GIULIANI. I had actually violated a rule of the Justice Department in using the word "mafia."

I said, well, punish me, because there is a mafia, and it has an organizing principle. You know what that principle is? Being Italian. That is the principle.

When there were a bunch of car thefts in southern Brooklyn, I didn't go look for Hispanics or Asians or blacks. I went and looked for Italian kids, because they were doing all the car thefts. That was profiling, but if I hadn't profiled, I wouldn't have caught them.

There are two kinds of profiling: Profiling based on hard facts that lead you to the criminal or criminal group or criminal enterprise here, jihad, or profiling just for the purpose of harming some particular group that is doing nothing wrong. So I think we have to define this word carefully.

I think that political correctness has cost us lives. I do not think the attack at Fort Hood would have occurred if we had not been applying political correctness, and I think those brave people would be alive today. I think they died because of political correctness, because no one was paying attention to what was being written by the captain, in which he was predicting what he was doing. In fact, he was promoted even though his colleagues were saying that he had become very extreme, erratic, and a big exponent of jihad. I think he was not penalized, and promoted, because the people in the military were afraid that they would be accused of picking on people of a certain group.

Mr. KATKO. Thank you, Mr. Mayor.

Chairman McCAUL. Miss Rice is recognized.

Miss RICE. Thank you, Mr. Chairman.

Mr. Mayor, given your service as mayor to this great city of ours and your professional work since that time, how prepared do you think New York and this country are to handle a large-scale cyber attack? That is probably one of the more inevitable attacks that we have to look at. In your opinion.

Mr. GIULIANI. Not as well prepared as we are for the more traditional attacks.

New York City is—and, again, Commissioner Bratton I would defer to, and he can explain it. But, from a long time ago, New York City has constantly increased under different commissioners its response to terrorism. New York City Police Department is doing a lot of work, as is the FBI, in cybersecurity.

But, as a Nation, we are way behind in cybersecurity, way behind, because it can't be solved by the Government alone. American businesses have to spend a lot more money protecting themselves than they do.

If you are the CEO of a large company that is publicly traded, your expenditures for cybersecurity come out of your profit and loss. It means a million dollars, $10 million, $100 million, and you show less profit in that quarter. There is no countervailing benefit that you get for it. It isn't like hiring 50 people and they are productive and you can put something on the other side of the column.

American businesses, No. 1, have not spent enough time or money on developing cybersecurity, and, No. 2, the methods and techniques that we use, in many cases, are contradictory. Not everyone works with each other. People don't want to share intellectual property. There are many problems in the area that you are talking about that have not received the same attention that the other things we talked about earlier—the physical security.

That could be an area where this committee could play a big role in encouraging not only our Government, as we saw the vulnerability of the Internal Revenue Service—my goodness, that is frightening. It is absolutely frightening that someone can come in and get documents from the Internal Revenue Service. So I would say that is an area, maybe, where this committee should put some really great emphasis.

One of the big mistakes we make, I think, is we prepare for the next attack as if it is going to be the same as the last attack. What they are trying to do is trying to figure out some kind of new attack.

I think we have been forewarned about cybersecurity, so I am very glad you brought it up. I think it is something that should be given a great deal more attention by both the Government and the private sector.

Miss RICE. Thank you, Mr. Mayor.

Chairman MCCAUL. I thank the gentlelady.

Mr. Hurd is recognized.

Mr. HURD. Thank you, Mr. Chairman and Ranking Member, for holding this.

Mr. Mayor, thanks for being here today and your leadership during a difficult time.

I would also like to thank the city of New York for hosting us. I am from Texas, and Texans and New Yorkers have a lot in common. You know, we are proud of our heritage, we have a bunch of great accents, and, you know, we are not afraid to fight for our country.

This is the second time I have tried to be here. The first time I tried to come to this great facility, there were so many people here it was hard to get into. So that warms my heart, to know that there are many folks that are not going to forget what happened on those days of September 11.

This is special to me because I spent 9 years as an undercover officer in the CIA. Mr. Mayor, you talked about Yemen. The day I left San Antonio, Texas, to start training in the CIA was the day of the Cole explosion. You know, we did not take seriously what our enemies were saying then. You alluded to that in your opening remarks. We weren't taking seriously what was being said in the late 1980s either. It is unfortunate, I am not nervous that we are not going to take seriously, or we are not taking serious enough, some of the concerns we are hearing all over the world from our current enemies.

I have chased al-Qaeda all over the world—in India, Pakistan, and Afghanistan. They are a real threat. ISIS's ability to leverage social media is shocking. But one of the things that we have to do is we have to stop it where they live.

You know, since you have been out of elected office, you have been a leader in emergency preparedness, public safety, leadership during crisis. You have been described as turning an ungovernable city into one of the world-wide examples of good governance and an effective management. You have done deals all over the world, so I am going to refer to you as a deal-maker.

I have two questions, one on ISIS, one on Iran.

What else should we be doing in these places like Syria, in some of these cities, to help them stop this fight, stop this scourge in their tracks?

No. 2, my second question on Iran: As a deal-maker, usually, when you do a deal, people benefit on both sides of the deal. I am still having a difficult time figuring out how the United States benefits from this Iranian deal. I would love your insights on that.

Mr. GIULIANI. Well, on the second, I would refer you to Donald Trump, "Art of the Deal." He would probably give a much more interesting answer that would get you much more coverage for this committee.

But, on the second question, I think we were completely out-negotiated. If you just go back and look at what the premise of this negotiation was supposed to be, we lost on all those points.

This all began, you know, 10 years ago with U.N. resolutions that Iran would be non-nuclear. It wouldn't have any nuclear—any nuclear power. For the reason that I stated, you would have to be an idiot to think they need nuclear facilities in a country that is oil-rich and natural-gas-rich. They don't need the peaceful use of nuclear power.

So the premise of the original resolution was a non-nuclear Iran. We gave that away with a preliminary agreement when we began the negotiation with, how nuclear should Iran be?

So what do we get back for that? The release of prisoners? An Iran that is going to give up being devoted to the destruction of Israel? An Iran that is going to give up being devoted to the death of Americans? An Iran that is going to stop funding Hezbollah, Hamas, the Houthis, and about 12 other groups that don't even have names yet? We didn't get anything back for that.

Then we were going to have the Ronald Reagan "trust but verify." Well, we are just trusting; we are not verifying it.

First of all, we are consigning it to the IAEA. The IAEA was fooled twice by Iran before, in 2003 and 2005. The Fordow facility—I have forgotten the names of the other, actually, three facilities discovered by the MEK that the IAEA missed. I am sorry, I wouldn't trust them. I am a baseball fan. Three strikes and you are out.

"Trust but verify" to Ronald Reagan meant we verify—we, the United States. We go in and we make sure that they are not hiding nuclear material like they did before.

If anybody took the time to read Rouhani's memoirs, the reform Prime Minister of Iran, Rouhani brags in his memoirs that he fooled us twice before. He brags about it. It is astounding to me that we are trusting him.

Then we are giving them 24 days—which, by the way, as a lawyer, having read the agreement, I could probably extend it to 6 months, because you can appeal. It is not us that raises the objection; it is the IAEA, who got fooled twice before—actually, three times before.

I am trying to figure out what we're getting out of this. We are getting out of this the promise that they are not going to become nuclear for 10 or 15 years. If you believe that, there is a bridge right near here I am willing to sell you. So, as a dealmaker teaching Dealmaking 101, I would give us an F.

But that is no different than our reset of our relationship with Russia when we gave up the nuclear defense of the Czech Republic and Poland. What did we get in return for it? How about nothing? I would not sell my house for nothing. I would get something in return. Maybe if we had stuck to the nuclear defense of the Czech Republic and Poland, Crimea may never have happened.

So I see a one-sided deal completely in favor of Iran. I see, worse than that, an Iranian empire developing——

Mr. HURD. Thank you.

Mr. GIULIANI [continuing]. With Iraq and Syria and Yemen.

Mr. HURD. Thank you.

Chairman MCCAUL. Mr. Ratcliffe is recognized.

Mr. RATCLIFFE. Thank you, Chairman McCaul, for holding this hearing at this hallowed ground where nearly 14 years ago to the day America did look directly into the face of evil, an evil that took from us thousands of innocent lives in the most senseless and cowardly act of terrorism that the world has ever known. The evil of radical Islamic extremism changed the world that day. It changed the lives of everyone here in this room.

For me, personally, it compelled me to become a terrorism prosecutor and later the U.S. attorney. For that reason, I know all too well what the radical Islamic terrorists remain capable of today. They will not stop, they will not relent, they will not give up in their quest to destroy the American way of life.

We are here today in recognition of the fact that we, therefore, must remain ever-vigilant of the threat of radical Islamic extremism and those that seek to cause us harm.

But here in this place, which will always serve as a somber reminder of the lives lost and a somber reminder of just how fragile our freedoms are, so, too, must this place always be a reminder of the heroic efforts of so many of our police, our fire departments, rescue personnel, and volunteer citizens who stood up in a historic time of need for this Nation.

I include you in that group, Mayor Giuliani. Your leadership in the aftermath of 9/11 was something that not just this city but the entire country needed to rebuild and to persevere. It has been said and written by many that we all became New Yorkers at that time, and, in that respect, you became the mayor to all of us. I know I join everyone here and everyone around the country in telling you that we will forever remain grateful for your leadership.

I came prepared today, as the Chairman of this committee's Subcommittee on Cybersecurity, Infrastructure Protection, and Security Technologies, to ask you your opinions on that. You have given your comments and answered most of the important questions that I came here to ask. So, out of respect for the second panel and respect for your time, I will just say thank you and yield back the balance of my time.

Mr. GIULIANI. Thank you very much, Mr. Ratcliffe. Let me just say two things very, very briefly.

First of all, thank you very much for the compliments about leadership, but I would point out that I rested on the shoulders of giants, that whatever credit I get for leadership, there were hundreds and hundreds of people that were equally as heroic and more so than I was. It was from them that I derived my ability to move forward and do whatever I could to do. So the credit doesn't belong to me; it belongs to all of them.

Thank you for your interest in cybersecurity because I do believe that, as Congresswoman Rice pointed out, this is the great threat that we face in the future, and it is the one that we are not paying as much attention to as we should.

Mr. RATCLIFFE. Thank you.

Chairman MCCAUL. Mr. Donovan.

Mr. DONOVAN. Thank you, Mr. Chairman.

Mr. Mayor, when you are the most junior Member of a committee, by the time the questioning gets to you, you ask the witness what their favorite pizzeria is, and I already know yours.

You were not only America's mayor, you were not only the mayor of New York City, you were my mayor. For all the people on this panel, I was a resident of New York City during your mayoralty, and I very much appreciate what you have done for this city, what you continue to do.

Since that time, you have traveled throughout the country for the last 14 years. I remember calling a friend of mine from a different part of our country after the tragedy that happened right here and told them, wasn't it an amazing feeling to see all these cars with American flags flying on them, how people have come together? He said to me, what flags? There weren't flags flying from cars where he lived.

Some people at that time—although we talked about the heroics of people from other cities coming to help us, a lot of people looked at this as an attack on New York and not an attack on America.

This coming Friday, you and I will be going to many, many events in our city to continue our pledge that we will never forget. I am wondering, through your travels throughout the country, have people forgotten?

Mr. GIULIANI. Yes, some people have forgotten. But, you know, Dan, it is in the nature of just the human being that, as you move further and further away from an event, like the death of a loved one, you don't forget, but the impact of it isn't as great. Of course, the closer you are to an event, like, whether you are a New Yorker or you had friends in New York or—so I think it is the job of this committee to remind people of that.

I want to conclude by commending this committee, from the day of this inception to today, Mr. King, Mr. McCaul, all of the Democratic Members, all of the Republican Members, I think you have been one of the most effective committees in Congress in the things that you have done. I think you have been one of the most effective in being able to forge bipartisan solutions where you could.

I ask you, in closing, to please consider once again the legislation to make this a National memorial. Because this will serve to remind all Americans when we forget. Because I think that, unfortunately, this is going to be a war we are going to be in for a long time. So we have to keep reminding Americans of what is happening, because it is so subtle and it is so sometimes hard for them to see.

Those of you who have been in it in some capacity or another know it. But it is the job of this committee and it is the job of this museum to make sure that the American people remain vigilant so, if it does happen again, it doesn't happen because we weren't paying attention.

Thank you.

Chairman MCCAUL. Mr. Clawson is recognized.

Mr. CLAWSON. Got time for one more?

Mr. GIULIANI. Of course.

Mr. CLAWSON. All right.

First, I want to thank you for your service and for your bravery.

Now, according to my economic understanding, the U.S. economy is about $16 trillion, maybe a little more. We are over 20 percent of the global GDP. We are the engine of everyone else's economic growth, I think you would agree. Fifty billion dollars of trade deficit, roughly, every single month.

I think that if China or the European community, just as two examples, had to choose between doing business with Iran and selling a product at Walmart or Target, what do you think they would decide? When I hear that this was a bipolar decision between this deal and war, I wonder what happened to our economy that is the growth engine for the whole world?

Then, Mr. Mayor, I take it another step and say: We have a financial system—you may know better than me. How many billions of dollars just in arbitrage and hedges take place every day across continents?

The way that foreign corrupt-practices law works is, if somebody does something wrong and they put their money into our financial system, they get nabbed quick, correct?

Mr. GIULIANI. Correct.

Mr. CLAWSON. Yet, to my knowledge, in the Iranian deal, we have not used this awesome power of our being the center of the global financial system in the leverage for the deal. I am astounded that these facts are never really talked about and that we are making a deal that is based on verification without using the global economic leverage that seems so self-obvious. I must be missing something here.

I am not trying to run anybody down, in particular, but I think that this idea that the sanctions would fall apart is only because we don't want to use our financial system or our global economic power.

Am I missing something here, or would you agree with this different take on the Iranian outcome?

Mr. GIULIANI. I have not just grave reservations about the agreement; the agreement is, to me, frightening because we get so little in return, if anything, and we are creating an empire. We are making available to a country that is set on the destruction of our greatest ally, a country that is dedicated to killing Americans and continues to say that as they negotiate with us, we are making billions of dollars available to them.

Everyone on this panel and everyone of any political party would agree that Iran is the biggest sponsor of terrorism in the world, state sponsor of terrorism in the world. There is no disagreement about that. Why, in God's name, would you give them billions of dollars?

What does it mean to be a state sponsor of terrorism? It means you take money and you give it to terrorists. It means you take weapons and you give it to terrorists. It means, if you are a nuclear power, you take nuclear capacity and give it to terrorists.

One of the main reasons that these resolutions began was not just a fear that Iran would attack Israel with missiles; it was the fear that, if Iran had nuclear capacity, it would hand it off to the terrorists that it is presently sponsoring and we could have a dirty bomb in New York or in Chicago or in London or in Paris. Somehow we have forgotten that.

Iran should have no nuclear capacity. They cannot be trusted with nuclear capacity. Could we have used our economic power to stop it? Absolutely. Absolutely.

Finally, when you say the only alternative is war, you make it clear that you will not go to war, which maybe would have been the greatest leverage of all if the military option had not only been kept on the table but maybe the military option were something they were afraid of.

To win a negotiation, you need leverage. We gave away our leverage when we backed off that red line 12 times, because the Ayatollah took the measure of his opponent, and he took the measure of his opponent as, "I don't have to worry about a military response."

Chairman MCCAUL. Mayor, let me just close by saying that there were many heroes that day, that fateful, tragic day, and you, sir, were the leader. You are America's mayor. On behalf of a grateful Nation, I just want to personally say, on behalf of the committee, thank you so much for your service.

Mr. GIULIANI. Thank you very much for coming here and reminding everyone of what happened and for your continuing work for the security of our country, which I think is just about the best in the United States Congress.

Thank you.

[Applause.]

Chairman MCCAUL. In the interest of time, we will move to the second panel. Let me quickly introduce the next panel.

First, we have Commissioner William Bratton, currently serving as the 42nd police commissioner for the city of New York. He previously served as commissioner of the Boston Police Department and the Los Angeles Police Department.

Next, we have Commissioner Daniel Nigro, who currently serves as the 33rd commissioner of the New York Fire Department, joining in 1969. He has held every uniformed rank within the department during his 32-year career, including chief of the department following the attacks of September 11.

Next, we have Mr. Ielpi, who serves as the president of the September 11th Families Association and is a member of the Vigilant Fire Department in Great Neck, New York, where he became a volunteer in 1963 and rose to the position of chief of the department. On September 11, he helped organize operations at Ground Zero until midnight and returned to the site daily to assist in the rescue of the operations. He continued his work for 9 months to ensure all who were lost were returned home, including his own son, Jonathan, who was in the Squad 288.

Finally, we have Mr. Gregory Thomas, served as president of the National Organization of Black Law Enforcement Executives, serves as the senior executive for law enforcement operations in the Office of the Kings County District Attorney, where he is the principal liaison to New York City Police Department.

The witnesses' full written statements will appear in the record.

The Chair now recognizes Commissioner Bratton.

STATEMENT OF WILLIAM J. BRATTON, COMMISSIONER, NEW YORK POLICE DEPARTMENT

Mr. BRATTON. Good morning, Chairman McCaul and distinguished Members of this committee. My name is William J. Bratton. I am the police commissioner for the city of New York. On behalf of Mayor Bill de Blasio, I welcome you to New York City and to this 9/11 Memorial and Museum.

The location of these hearings could not be more appropriate. This site was hallowed by the lives we lost in the terrible attack that happened here. It was consecrated by those who sacrificed here, whose heroism here kept those losses smaller than they could have been. It has been dedicated, through the Memorial and Museum, to a promise: We will never yield in our efforts to prevent another event from happening here or anywhere else in this great city.

As you know, in 3 days, we will see the 14th anniversary of the September 11 attacks. In those 14 years, the New York City Police Department has changed dramatically. The traditional realm of municipal policing—the prevention of crime and disorder and the fostering of public approval—was expanded to include keeping the city and its people safe from terrorism.

This morning, I will provide a brief overview of the current terrorism threat environment and describe some of the NYPD's counterterrorism measures that are constantly evolving and expanding. I provided more extensive written testimony to the committee, as well.

In many respects, we currently face a greater likelihood of attack than we have seen in years. With regard to crime, New York City

just experienced the safest summer in 25 years, but, with regard
to the current terrorism threat environment, we now face multiple
hazards: Known wolves and lone wolves, as my deputy commissioner of intelligence and counterterrorism, John Miller, says; al-
Qaeda, particularly al-Qaeda in the Arabian Peninsula, or AQAP,
which operates primarily out of Yemen. It remains a distinct
threat. They are believed to be the primary driver of the terrible
attack in Paris at Charlie Hebdo.

But we have also seen the emergence a new virulent player,
ISIL, or ISIS, or the Islamic State of Iraq in the Levant. By establishing a pseudo-state in the war-torn no man's land between Iraq
and Syria, ISIL has fundamentally destabilized the Middle East
and many other parts of the world.

Fortunately, its direct impact has not yet been felt here, but the
important words there are "direct impact" and "yet," because ISIL
has been far more successful than al-Qaeda at driving indirect impacts. ISIL has shunned al-Qaeda's model, which focuses on se-
cretly recruiting and training small cells for the next grand attack.
Instead, they have embraced a diffuse, lone-wolf model which
mass-markets the global call for violence in the name of the so-
called Islamic state.

ISIL promises that those who carry out this carnage will be publicly revered on global social media. They will be remembered as
heroic fighters who are an essential part of a larger struggle. This
promise of valor, belonging, and empowerment has a particular appeal to those who fall in the margins of society, those who are failing at most other things in life. ISIL is focused on attacks that require minimal capability, low-tech, low-cost, and high-impact, because killing with a gun or a car or a simply-made IED is something even those who fail at most other things unfortunately can
do.

Most Americans, either most New Yorkers, don't know that the
law enforcement and counterterrorism intelligence communities
have been remarkably busy recently. In June alone, several men
were arrested in New York, New Jersey, and Boston for taking part
in ISIL-driven plots being pushed over social media platforms.
These recent plots, most uncovered by the FBI–NYPD Joint Terrorism Task Force, ranged from a plot to behead a New York-based
critic after a failed attack at an event in Garland, Texas, to plots
that involved building pressure-cooker bombs in the days leading
up to New York's Fourth of July fireworks celebration.

This wave of arrests comes after the JTTF arrested two New
York City women in April, women who were in the process of re-
searching explosive compounds to construct an IED. Among the
targets they discussed for their bomb plot was a police funeral for
officers killed in the line of duty. I am proud to say that I was able
to meet and thank the undercover New York City police detective
who spent more than a year on this case and was a lynchpin in
that investigation.

None of these plots, had they gone forward, would have had the
scope of the attacks that happened here. In that respect, today's
plots do not have the depth of those we face from al-Qaeda, even
at its strongest. But while the threat from terrorist groups is not

as deep, it has grown now to be miles-wide, indeed world-wide, and, in many ways, harder to track.

After the worst terrorist attack in New York history, New York City certainly proved its resilience. But any terrorist attack against this city, regardless of scale, would have a profound effect—here, across the country, and throughout the world.

That is why, even with the significant funding for Department of Homeland Security and its appropriators in Congress, the NYPD continues to invest our own resources in this fight.

During the Charlie Hebdo attacks in Paris, we saw police driven back, even coldly executed, by terrorists with superior weapons and endless ammunition. An NYPD team flew to Paris and was fully briefed on all the lessons learned there. Another team of NYPD Emergency Service Unit officers and hostage negotiators went to Sydney, Australia, after an ISIL acolyte took hostages in a downtown cafe in Sydney. When ISIL-driven attacks occurred in the Bardo museum, our detective assigned to Interpol traveled to Tunisia.

The collective lessons learned from these attacks formed our plans for the recently formed Strategic Response Group, or SRG. SRG is an 800-person unit, soon-to-be 800-person unit, specially equipped and trained to deal with crowd management but also terrorist-threat, active-shooter types of activity.

We have also recently formed the Critical Response Command, CRC, which will take an interim initiative that was put in place by Commissioner Kelly shortly after 9/11 and now institutionalize it in our Counterterrorism Bureau—415 highly-trained officers also specially equipped and trained to constantly deal with the growing threat that I have referenced.

SRG and CRC are significant city-wide units, an additional 1,200 officers that we will be focusing as part of the responsibilities on the growing threat.

We also, within the past year, assigned 250 detectives to a new initiative that includes significantly increasing our capabilities to deal with cybersecurity threats both in the traditional crime world as well as the counterterrorism world.

We have, within the last month, assigned a squad of detectives to the FBI to work with them on an expanding cybersecurity initiative that they have recently created. Within the next several weeks, I will be assigning another squad of detectives to District Attorney Cy Vance's office as he significantly expands, in the financial capital of the world, his efforts to deal with cybersecurity threats to our financial institutions.

New York City remains in the cross-hairs of global terrorism. Since September 11, 2001, there have been more than 20 terrorist plots against New York City, including those discussed above. So far, they have been thwarted at nearly every turn by the efforts of the NYPD and our local and Federal partners. That partnership, by the way, is stronger than it ever has been.

Under Deputy Commissioner John Miller, the honored investigative reporter who was one of the first to interview Osama bin Laden when he began to make his threats against the United States, and then a veteran of the FBI, the LAPD's Counterterrorism Bureau, and the Office of the Director of National Intelligence, and now my counterterrorism intelligence director, we have undergone a collaborative reset with the vast variety of agencies, entities, and services with which we work every day.

Together, we have continued to keep this city safe, and we have done so while upholding the Constitutional rights accorded to those who live, work, and visit New York City. Protecting civil liberties is as important as protecting our city. After all, it is our freedom that makes us a target for those who hate us.

Mindful that a more detailed version of this testimony has been submitted and aware of the committee's mandate, I would like to thank you for inviting me to testify. I will be happy to answer any questions that the committee and its Members may have. Thank you.

[The prepared statement of Mr. Bratton follows:]

PREPARED STATEMENT OF WILLIAM J. BRATTON

SEPTEMBER 8, 2015

Good morning, Chairman McCaul and distinguished Members of the committee. My name is William J. Bratton, police commissioner of the city of New York. On behalf of Mayor Bill de Blasio, welcome to New York City and to the 9/11 Memorial and Museum.

The location of these hearings could not be more appropriate. This site was hallowed by the lives we lost in the terrible attack that happened here. It was consecrated by those who sacrificed here, and whose heroism here kept those losses smaller than they could have been. It has been dedicated, through the memorial and museum, to a promise: We will never yield in our efforts to prevent another event from happening here, or anywhere else in this city.

As you know, in 3 days we will see the 14th anniversary of the September 11 attacks. In those 14 years, the New York City Police Department has changed dramatically. The traditional realm of municipal policing—the prevention of crime and disorder, and the fostering of public approval—was expanded to include keeping the city and its people safe from terrorism. This morning I will provide an overview of the current terrorism threat environment and the NYPD's counterterrorism measures.

In many respects, we currently face a greater likelihood of attack than we have seen in years. With regard to crime, we just experienced the safest summer in 25 years, with murders and shootings at modern lows. But with regard to the current terrorism threat environment, we now face multiple hazards: "Known wolves and lone wolves," as my Deputy Commissioner of Intelligence and Counterterrorism John Miller says.

Al-Qaeda, particularly al-Qaeda in the Arabian Peninsula, or AQAP, which operates primarily out of Yemen, remains a distinct threat. They are believed to be the primary driver of the terrible attack in Paris at Charlie Hebdo.

But we have also seen the emergence of a new, virulent player—ISIL, or the Islamic State of Iraq and the Levant. By establishing a pseudo-state in the war-torn no-man's land between Iraq and Syria, ISIL has fundamentally destabilized the Middle East. Fortunately, its direct impact has not yet been felt here. But the important words there are "direct impact" and "yet." Because ISIL has been far more successful than al-Qaeda at driving indirect impacts. ISIL has shunned al-Qaeda's model, which focuses on the next grand attack. Instead, they have embraced a diffuse, "lone wolf" model, which encourages unaffiliated independent operators to do whatever damage they can with whatever is at hand.

This threat is decentralized and much harder to detect than threats orchestrated by al-Qaeda. ISIL's alarmingly effective messaging—as refined as anything found on Madison Avenue or in Hollywood—reaches marginalized, solitary actors. These are terrorists who largely operate outside the kind of command-and-control systems, or cells, that we have learned to penetrate and dismantle. In the past year, we have seen many such attacks around the world, prompted by ISIL videos. Last October, here in New York City, an ax-wielding, radicalized malcontent attacked four of our officers in broad daylight, seriously injuring two. He was the human equivalent of an unguided missile: Launched remotely by messages directed at disaffected people on the fringes, people with a lot of anger and little to lose. There were similar attacks in Canada and Australia.

Despite this, we have not wavered in our efforts. One example is the arrest, made by the FBI–NYPD Joint Terrorism Task Force (JTTF) in April, of two Queens residents who sought to make bombs like the ones used at the Boston Marathon is an example. That case was begun by an NYPD source and centered on an Intelligence Bureau undercover officer. Then in June and August, a group of men from Queens, Staten Island, and New Jersey were arrested by the JTTF for conspiring to join ISIL and for conspiring to carry out a terrorist attack in the New York City region.

These cases and others demonstrate that New York City remains in the crosshairs of global terrorism. Since September 11, 2001, there have been more than 20 terrorist plots against New York City, targeting the New York Stock Exchange, Citigroup headquarters, the Brooklyn Bridge, John F. Kennedy Airport, Times Square, Ground Zero, the subway system, major synagogues, and even NYPD funerals. So far, they have been thwarted at nearly every turn by the efforts of the NYPD and our local and Federal partners. That partnership, by the way, is stronger than is has ever been. Under Deputy Commissioner Miller, a veteran of the FBI and the Office of the Director of National Intelligence, we have undergone a collaborative reset with the vast variety of agencies, entities, and services with which we work. Together, we have kept this city safe—and we have done so while upholding the Constitutional rights and liberties accorded to those who live, work, and visit New York City.

To accomplish this, I have been fortunate to build on the work of my predecessor, Police Commissioner Raymond W. Kelly. To his great credit, he recognized that the NYPD could not defer its counterterrorism responsibility to others, and he set about reorganizing the Department accordingly.

Soon after 2001, the NYPD became the first police department in the country to develop its own robust counterterrorism capacity. At the time, we had already been in the Joint Terrorism Task Force for two decades, having co-founded the JTTF with the FBI here in New York. We had an intelligence division that focused on crime and protecting the many dignitaries and world leaders who come to New York, particularly during the United Nations General Assembly—the 70th Session of which is just weeks away. But the murder here of more than 2,700 people on a single morning meant that the Department's efforts had to be redoubled.

We established a division responsible for training and equipping every one of our police officers for counterterrorism duties. Our intelligence mission grew to include gathering and analyzing intelligence with global implications. In these expansions, our personnel were our premier resource. Over the years, the caliber of people we have been able to attract has played a major role in our ability to protect New York.

We have hired civilian intelligence analysts who are experts in intelligence and foreign affairs. They study terrorist groups, trends, and methods of attack.

We have assigned police officers to serve as liaisons in 12 cities around the world: London, Madrid, Paris, Tel Aviv, Abu Dhabi, Amman, Lyon, Montreal, Toronto, Singapore, Santo Domingo, and Sydney. From these locations, and in coordination with our Federal and international partners, our liaisons can travel to the scenes of terrorist attacks that occur throughout Europe, the Middle East, Africa, and Asia to help analyze the specific tactics used, the type of weaponry and explosives involved, where the planning was conducted, and the nature of the targets—all to better learn how best to defend New York City against a similar attack.

The liaisons are funded primarily by the New York Police Foundation, and their investment has paid dividends. Our liaison in France gave us real-time updates on the situation police confronted during the Charlie Hebdo attacks. After attacks at the Bardo Museum, we sent liaisons to Tunis and obtained on-the-ground intelligence. In 2013, our detectives deployed to the scene of the Westgate Mall in Kenya following the heinous attack by al-Qaeda's Somalia-based affiliate al-Shabaab. In response to the 2012 deadly bus attack at the airport in Bulgaria, our liaison officer stationed in Tel Aviv was able to supply us with critical information on the tactics used by the attackers. The NYPD uses the information gathered from such assignments to adapt its tactics, techniques, and procedures to deter and/or thwart potential similar attacks in New York City.

Our personnel's remarkable ethnic and national diversity affords us a deep pool of foreign-language-speaking officers. This has allowed us to build a foreign-linguist program with more than 1,200 registered speakers of 85 different languages—Arabic, Dari, Farsi, Mandarin, Pashto, Russian, Spanish, and Urdu, to name just a few.

Our diversity has bolstered every aspect of our mission, from counterterrorism to crime fighting to community relations. Through our Community Affairs Bureau, we have assigned officers to the Arab and Muslim, Chinese, Eastern European, Hispanic, and West African communities who are actually part of those communities. The connections they make ensure that the community shares the responsibility for counterterrorism. It's a force multiplier when it comes to keeping the city safe. To facilitate this shared responsibility, we established "New York City Safe," a terrorism-threat hotline, where concerned citizens can report suspicious activity.

In addition to our community outreach efforts, we also coordinate closely with outside partners, including the Federal Government, regional law enforcement agencies, and the private sector. We continue to work hand-in-glove with the JTTF, sharing information and following up on terrorism-related leads. We also assign personnel to the Drug Enforcement Administration's Special Operations Division, the High Intensity Drug Trafficking Area Task Force, the National Intelligence Council, and U.S. Customs and Border Protection.

Through a program called Operation Sentry, we also share information with more than 150 law enforcement agencies throughout the Northeast and Mid-Atlantic. We conduct various types of training with our Sentry partners, hold video-conferences on emerging threats, and exchange best practices with respect to terrorist and traditional crime matters. These collaborations are utterly necessary in a world where terrorists—and criminals—ignore the borders and boundaries that limit us. Terrorists frequently develop their plot outside their target areas. In 2005, the suicide bombers who struck the London transit system built their bombs in Leeds, 180 miles north of the target. Closer to home, the first World Trade Center bombing in 1993 was planned across the Hudson River, in New Jersey. Faisal Shahzad, who attempted to detonate a car bomb in Times Square in 2010, assembled his explosives in Connecticut.

For an understanding of how important collaboration in these matters is, look no further than Shahzad's comment to the officers who removed him from a plane at JFK minutes before he might have escaped: "I was expecting you—are you NYPD or FBI?" The answer was neither—they were Customs officers. In the task of keeping us safe, everyone has a role to play.

We collaborate with the private sector, as well—there are nearly 13,000 members of the region's private security industry who participate in a program called "NYPD Shield." The membership consists of security professionals tasked with protecting critical infrastructure and sensitive buildings in the New York metropolitan area. Through the Shield program, we regularly host conferences, sector-specific briefings, and training seminars as well as share NYPD strategic assessments on terror trends. Under another initiative, Operation Nexus, our detectives have made over 55,000 visits to businesses that make, sell, or inventory products, services, or materials that might be exploited by terrorists, such as truck rental outfits, fertilizer stores, and chemical supply companies. We ask them to contact us if they see anything unusual, anything that gives them pause.

Having the right personnel and partnerships is part of the equation, but monetary resources are required, as well. Since 2002, the Department has been awarded $1.4 billion in Federal counterterrorism funds, which have been used for mission-critical equipment, training, and salaries. In this respect, Department of Homeland Security grants and other disbursements have played an integral role in protecting the 8.5 million people who call New York City home, the millions more who live in and work in the greater metropolitan area, and the 56 million visitors we have each year.

Over the past several years, the "Securing the Cities" program has spent more than $21 million installing radiation detection equipment throughout neighboring jurisdictions and at key points of entry into the five boroughs. Across the city, we have distributed approximately 3,000 radiation pagers to units throughout the department and nearly 4,000 radiological dosimeters to each Patrol Borough's counterterrorism trailer. Even as this funding to the greater New York City region is being reduced, the NYPD continues to invest heavily in acquiring and maintaining state-of-the-art equipment to identify, prevent, or disrupt threats. From sonar systems to thermal imaging cameras, we have installed highly-sensitive detection equipment on the boats and helicopters we use to patrol New York Harbor. Police vehicles are also outfitted with similar detection capabilities.

We have also benefited from DHS grants in developing our Domain Awareness System, or DAS. Over the past 6 years, approximately $325,000,000 has been expended, primarily through multiple DHS grants. When DAS is fully implemented, New York City will be one of the most target-hardened cities in the Nation, with more than 6,600 closed-circuit television cameras (CCTVs) and nearly 500 license-plate-recognition readers (LPRs) on every bridge and tunnel coming into and leaving Manhattan. High-definition CCTVs with thermal-imaging capability are already mounted on helicopters and mobile LPRs are deployed in both marked and nondescript vehicles to aid in the tracking and interdiction of suspect vehicles, allowing for a rapid response to major incidents. Where DAS really opens new horizons, however, is in its data collection. All sensor data will be correlated with records data from NYPD and external databases, and contextual alerts will be provided to users.

Geographic analytic mode capabilities will support pattern identification among disparate data types. The DAS project also continues to expand as additional capabilities, functions, and sensors of various forms (CCTV, CBRN, etc.) are integrated.

Additionally, thanks to funding from the Mayor and the Manhattan District Attorney's Office, the NYPD is implementing its "Mobile Digital Initiative." Mobile Digital puts a smart phone in every uniformed officer's hands and a smart tablet in every vehicle. The Project is ramping up and we expect to see steady-state deployments beginning in August, with a completion date of February 2016. These devices will be DAS compatible, making every one of the NYPD's 35,000 officers a counterterrorism asset.

We are also developing and implementing a robust cybersecurity program. Malicious software, data exfiltration, and exploits all take place in the virtual realm of a computer network. In order to monitor and mitigate such an attack, the NYPD must possess the appropriate sophisticated security tools. The Department's existing cybersecurity capabilities are not adequate to fully defend the Department in the current threat landscape. Accordingly, the NYPD has commenced the Total Network Visibility Initiative (TNVI), an innovative methodology utilizing a variety of reporting mechanisms such as log and packet inspection, net flows and edge monitoring, among other techniques. These techniques will allow network defenders to "see" the malicious action in cyber space, and take necessary actions to rapidly mitigate threats to NYPD Information Systems.

These personnel and resources are fully leveraged to apply the NYPD's counterterrorism measures.

We constantly seek to disrupt budding plots. Every day, through Operation Hercules, we deploy teams of heavily-armed officers to make unannounced visits to iconic locations.

We place particular emphasis on the subway system in light of its primacy as a target and because it is a vital artery that keeps this city running. In excess of 6 million New Yorkers use the subways every day. Protecting this system is one of our top priorities and greatest challenges. The system is designed to be open 24 hours a day, every day of the year. Its very strengths as mass transit leave it vulnerable to attack. After the bombing of the London transit system in 2005, we began screening the bags and backpacks of subway passengers. Every day, we maintain posts at each of the 14 underwater subway tunnels. Thanks to a Federal grant, we were able to hire over 100 police officers for our Transit Impact Program and reassign an equal number of veteran officers to our transit-based Anti-Terrorism Unit. They conduct mobile screenings, transit order maintenance sweeps, surges, and counter-surveillance. We have heightened uniformed patrols underground and conduct regular security sweeps of subway cars.

The salaries and overtime for all of the specialized counterterrorism teams described above, including those for detectives and analysts in the Intelligence Bureau and on the Joint Terrorism Task Force, accounted for more than $420 million of the Federal funds allocated to NYPD since 2002.

We also prioritize counterterrorism training. Since 2002, we have dedicated $100 million of Federal counterterrorism funds to training programs, including Behavioral Observation and Suspicious Activity Recognition; Hostile Surveillance Detection; Initial Law Enforcement Response to Suicide Bomber Attacks; Advanced Explosive Trace Detection; Awareness and Response to Biological Events; Chemical Ordinance, Biological and Radiological Awareness Training; and Maritime Incident Response Team Training.

The Department conducts and participates with other New York City and Government agencies in counterterrorism exercises including tabletop, functional, and full-scale (i.e. "boots on the ground") drills. The Department has taken part in dozens of major exercises to plan for and safeguard against chemical, biological, radiological, or nuclear attacks, in addition to another dozen workshops with our Securing the Cities regional partners. Utilizing lessons learned from previous terror attacks, including those garnered from our liaisons abroad, the Department holds regular exercises to examine potential threat scenarios and capabilities that will be required to successfully respond to and mitigate the threat.

In addition to those mentioned above, in the past year we have held active-shooter exercises, including one recently conducted just above us in the new World Trade Center Tower. We have conducted simulated IED attacks, staged various attack scenarios at high-profile events; and conducted exercises involving dirty bomb detonations at subway stations and platforms. These exercises inform our special event planning and response. For example, based on lessons learned the Department may deploy physical security measures such as temporary barriers; Critical Response Vehicles; heavy weapons teams; canine assets; bag screening; explosive trace detection; hostile surveillance detection; or radiation detection.

These are some of the tools we are using to keep pace with the evolving threat of terrorism. The philosophy behind them is simple: We have to develop the best intelligence available, expand our partnerships, and take protective measures to defeat whatever our adversaries might be planning next.

Because unfortunately, our adversaries have multiplied in recent years. As was discussed above, organized, well-equipped attacks like the one in Paris remain part of the threat picture, but we now face the diffuse threat of the ISIL-inspired lone wolf, as well. To address this new, more complicated reality, the NYPD is changing its Counterterrorism Critical Response Vehicle model.

Thanks to Mayor de Blasio, who authorized the first headcount expansion in more than a decade, we are getting 1,300 new officers. The staffing increase has allowed us to take what was a temporary deployment scheme and make a permanent Critical Response Command. Instead of drawing hundreds of officers from the patrol precincts randomly each day and depleting local patrol resources, the CRC will be staffed with dedicated personnel specially trained for the counterterrorism mission. On a day-to-day basis, they will protect a range of critical infrastructure and important sites. But they also provide support for our Emergency Services units and counter active-shooters, "lone wolf" attacks, or more sophisticated operations such as those in Paris or Mumbai. All personnel will have received advanced training in counterterrorism operations and will be equipped with highly-advanced and specialized equipment, such as explosive trace detection equipment and under-vehicle inspection systems.

Finally, I wish to assure the committee that our commitment to public safety and security does not trump our commitment to privacy and Constitutional protections. Protecting civil liberties is as important as protecting the city. After all, it is our freedom that makes us a target for those who hate it. Our terrorism-related investigations are treated with particular care because we recognize that they may, at times, implicate the First Amendment and other important issues. Accordingly, we abide not only by the U.S. Constitution and other applicable law, but also a Federal consent decree that imposes additional checks on our counterterrorism investigations.

Fourteen years after 9/11, New York enjoys the distinction of being the safest big city in America. It is also commercially vibrant, culturally diverse, and free. These successes are due, in no small measure, to the 50,000 uniformed and civilian members of the New York City Police Department, who, together with our partners, including the distinguished Members of this committee, have sought and strived and never yielded in keeping the city safe.

Thank you again for this opportunity to testify. I would be happy to answer any of your questions.

Chairman McCAUL. Thank you, Commissioner Bratton.

The Chairman recognizes Commissioner Nigro.

STATEMENT OF DANIEL A. NIGRO, COMMISSIONER, NEW YORK FIRE DEPARTMENT

Mr. NIGRO. Well, thank you. Good morning, Mr. Chairman and all the Members present. Thank you for having me here today.

Since I joined the FDNY in 1969, there has been a tremendous shift in the way we train and prepare the members of the FDNY. The department's primary mission has always been to protect life and property, but in the ever-changing threat environment of a post-9/11 world, that mission has become even more complex.

The department has confronted this challenge by building an infrastructure that identifies potential threats, builds a response plan, and trains members to carry out those plans.

The result is the FDNY is prepared at a moment's notice to provide rescue and triage in an infinite array of potential scenarios and disasters. Not only does this ensure we are prepared in the case of a terrorist event, but it also means the department functions as a robust regional asset that can be deployed in almost any kind of disaster scenario.

The value of this has been seen nationally, such as when the FDNY responded to New Orleans after Hurricane Katrina, as well as State-wide, as when we responded to the record snowstorm in Buffalo earlier this year.

These assets can also be utilized locally to prevent a crisis, such as when a case of the Ebola virus reached New York City. The FDNY was able to draw upon a preparedness framework combining training, resources, and drills that specialized units developed preparing for bioterrorism threats. This includes decontamination procedures and operating in chemical-protective clothing which, as an added benefit, also protects against bloodborne pathogens.

DHS funds helped build and train the Haz-Tac and Haz-Mat units that played a key role in the response and supported the purchase of specialized equipment and resources that provide emergency medical transport, treatment, and patient care.

The planning, training, and equipment the FDNY utilizes can be applied in any mass-casualty situation, whether a terrorist attack, natural disaster, industrial accident, pandemic outbreak, or biological event. This ensures that we are not only prepared to respond to likely scenarios but that we have the training and capability to respond to any threat presented to us, expected or not. This is not a capability the department had on 9/11, and our ability to build this capability has been largely as a result of the funding we have received from the Federal Government.

A perfect example of how even the day-to-day work of the FDNY is impacted by this training is the Times Square bombing attempt in 2010. Though first responders from Engine 54 and Ladder 4 initially responded to a typical fire call, once on the scene, they immediately recognized the threat potential of the smoking vehicle and ensured the appropriate law enforcement resources were called to the scene. They took action that day that reduced injuries, protected property, and saved lives.

This type of training is happening every day in the FDNY and is essential to our ability to serve the city of New York. By investing in core areas—planning, incident management, leadership, communications, patient triage and treatment, Haz-Mat, marine firefighting, and search and technical rescue—we are better prepared to adapt to a changing threat environment if disaster strikes. We have structured our core competencies to respond to routine and extreme events, including acts of terrorism.

Thank you again for the opportunity to speak here today on this important topic.

[The prepared statement of Mr. Nigro follows:]

PREPARED STATEMENT OF DANIEL A. NIGRO

SEPTMBER 8, 2015

The FDNY's primary mission is to protect life and property. The department carries out this mission through firefighting, search and rescue, pre-hospital patient care, and hazardous materials mitigation. The planning, training, and equipment mentioned below can be applied in any mass casualty situation, whether a terrorist attack, natural disaster, industrial accident, pandemic outbreak, or biological event.

PREPAREDNESS CORE VALUES

The department builds systems, like our Tiered Response System, which can be scaled and adapted to ensure the right mix of resources and expertise, depending on the type of incident or emergency. The department also builds systems of collaboration, partnering with other city agencies and regional responders to share lessons learned, and to develop interagency plans, protocols, and drills. Members of the department have acquired a tremendous amount of knowledge and know-how since 9/11, and this knowledge is helping the city plan and prepare for extreme hazards and emergencies. The department has also invested in specialized training facilities—revamping our Fire and EMS Academies—and environments, like our Shipboard Simulator and our Subway Simulator. These tools not only serve the FDNY, but are considered city and regional resources.

THE CENTER FOR TERRORISM AND DISASTER PREPAREDNESS

At the core of these preparedness efforts is the Center for Terrorism and Disaster Preparedness (CTDP). We created the Center in 2004 to be the focal point for the department's strategic preparedness, creating dynamic and practical approaches to counterterrorism, disaster response, and consequence management. The development of CTDP came out of the 9/11 McKinsey After Action Report (AAR).

The Center's core competencies include: Intelligence sharing, weapons of mass destruction (WMD) and security preparedness, exercise design, emergency response planning, education, strategy and technology.

Intelligence sharing.—The intelligence branch of the Center has expanded the FDNY's role to become an active producer of intelligence tailored to the needs of fire fighters and emergency responders. The department uses a PC and web-based communication tool—Diamond Plate—to deliver critical training and situational awareness content directly to firehouses and EMS stations in real-time. With firehouses and EMS stations located throughout the city, this tool has helped the department leverage technology to share information and to break down distances. In recent months, this platform has been a key resource to disseminate information to our first responders on Ebola and Legionnaires' Disease—videos, information, procedures and safety protocols—and to share messages with our entire workforce.

WMD and Security Preparedness.—The primary mission of the Center's WMD branch is to coordinate strategy and tactics, and share chemical, biological, radiological, nuclear, and explosive research. For example, we are currently working with the Department of Health and Mental Hygiene to collect, share, and map radiological data during radiation emergencies, which will allow our commanders in the field and at the FDOC to visualize contaminated areas. We have also strategically deployed a stockpile of WMD medical counter-measures in EMS stations and hospitals, and we also train and carry WMD antidote kits on every 9–1–1 ambulance and fire apparatus.

Exercise Design.—CTDP conducts workshops, tabletops, functional, and full-scale exercises to test the knowledge and efficacy of the Department's all-hazards response protocols. CTDP also makes recommendations on improvements in detailed after-action reports. The CTDP has partnered with the Department of Homeland Security (DHS), NYPD, NYC Office of Emergency Management, the West Point Combating Terrorism Leadership Center, and the Centers for Disease Control to plan and prepare exercises for natural, accidental, and terrorist events. On average, CTDP runs 35–40 preparedness exercises each year.

Emergency Preparedness.—The Center creates and updates emergency response plans to provide both general and detailed tactical direction for units responding to terrorist events and natural disasters. As part of this planning, the Center helps develop and maintain the FDNY's continuity of operations plans. This team has developed plans for the following events: Haz-Mat release, subway chemical attack, bio-response, improvised explosive device, collapse rescue, and hurricanes. As mentioned above, the department is also building systems of collaboration. An example of this is the work that the FDNY and the NYPD are doing to respond to a large-scale Active Shooter Mass Casualty Incident (MCI). The FDNY/NYPD have worked together to develop a "Response to Active-Shooter Incidents" emergency response plan, and have begun conducting drills on the plan.

One of our concerns is the use of fire as a weapon. The devastating 2008 attacks in Mumbai represent a game-changer. Over 3 days, a city of nearly 14 million was held hostage while 166 people were murdered in multiple locations, introducing a new model for terrorist attacks. The salient features of a Mumbai-style attack include multiple terrorists, multiple targets, and multiple modes of attack deployed over a prolonged operational period to amplify media attention. Despite all of the violence, the most iconic images from that event remain those of the Taj Mahal Hotel on fire. The pictures of people at the windows of the hotel trying to escape the flames are reminiscent of 9/11. Despite the striking images from that major attack, interest in using fire as either a strategic or a tactical weapon has not been well understood and largely ignored to date. However, it is a weapon that could significantly alter the dynamics of a terrorist attack. FDNY is working closely with NYPD, the FBI, and The Department of State's Diplomatic Security Services to develop the procedures for joint tactical teams—teams comprised of fire personnel and security forces operating together—in an environment with armed terrorists, fire and smoke, and mass casualties. All three agencies have been working with us in full-scale exercises at the Fire Academy and more are being planned.

SPECIAL OPERATIONS COMMAND

In addition to the extensive planning discussed above, the FDNY has significantly enhanced our Special Operations Command (SOC) capabilities, so that we are more prepared than ever to deal with incidents involving biological, chemical, or radioactive releases, major structural collapses, maritime operations, and other major incidents with mass-casualty potential.

The underpinning of these enhancements is the "Tiered Response System" that we established to ensure the optimal availability and distribution of response resources. This tiered-response framework entails training FDNY units in a variety of response capabilities at incremental proficiency levels and strategically locating those units across the city.

Let me illustrate this Tiered Response structure for hazardous material incidents. At the highest level—the Specialist Level—is our Hazardous Material Unit and Haz-Mat Battalion Chiefs who have over 600 hours of professional training and carry advanced instrumentations. The next level is comprised of 12 Haz-Mat Tech II Units and 39 Haz-Tac Ambulances. At the next level down we have 25 Haz-Mat Tech I Units, 25 Decontamination Engines and 29 Chemical Protective Clothing Ladder Companies who can operate in hazardous environments. At the foundation level, all fire and EMS personnel are trained on Haz-Mat/WMD operations. As you can see, our tiered response system provides a very robust structure for Haz-Mat response and mitigation.

Our collapse search-and-rescue members are structured in a similar manner and receive the highest levels of training the department offers in technical rescue and victim-removal, including more than 280 hours of specialized rescue training in collapse response and rescue operations.

Our Emergency Medical System, the largest in the United States, is also tiered, starting with certified first responders, EMTs, paramedics, specialized rescue medics, and Haz-Tac paramedics and Haz-Tac EMTs.

The FDNY's Tiered Response System allows the department to adapt to extreme events by creating Task Forces to give the city and the region highly-trained teams that can rapidly respond to large-scale hazards and emergencies.

ORGANIZATIONAL AND COMMUNICATIONS INFRASTRUCTURE

Of course, enhanced capabilities are only one component of our preparedness goals. The Department has also taken steps to improve our organizational and communications infrastructures as well. The Department has:
- Developed a fully-staffed and trained Incident Management Team (IMT), who played a key role in the Harlem and Second Avenue explosions.
- Launched an automated recall program that can target off-duty members to ensure resources are available to maintain coverage throughout the city during any emergency.
- Implemented a communications channel between on-scene firefighters and the EMS command.
- Implemented a second EMS city-wide channel to handle concurrent Multiple Casualty Incidents.
- Developed and launched a Suspicious Activity Reporting (SAR) information and awareness campaign in firehouses and EMS stations.
- Implemented the Fire-ground Accountability Program (FGAP), which consists of a number of inter-related applications to enhance fire-ground safety and accountability.
- We've made an investment in our workforce, providing senior Fire and EMS Officers with customized leadership and strategic-management training. This includes our Fire Officers Management Institute (FOMI)—partnering with GE and Columbia University—and our West Point Combatting Terrorism Leadership program. These programs help the Department build the next generation of leaders.

The Department has successfully deployed a three-part field communication system that represents a critical step in improved fire-ground communications. The system consists of 13 vehicle-based, cross-band repeaters, which allow radio signals to be transmitted into dense building environments; 75 high-powered portable command post radios; and pre-programmed handie-talkie radios with several customized features that have improved on-scene tactical and command communications and firefighter safety.

The FDNY has also built a state-of-the-art Emergency Operations Center at FDNY Headquarters to enhance information sharing, command-and-control communications, and on-scene situational awareness capabilities. The Department is also completing a redundant back-up facility on Staten Island, which will serve as a fully-functional back-up operations center where command-and-control personnel within the FDNY and first responders can plan, coordinate, and share relevant information with each other, and with other public safety agencies.

An element of this system is the concept of a Networked Command: Linking on-scene situational awareness capabilities with command-and-control-level operations at Emergency Operation Centers (EOC). Lastly, with the assistance of DHS and the Congressional Homeland Security Committee, FDNY has a secure room to receive and share Classified intelligence with DHS, the National Counterterrorism Center (NCTC), Fusion Centers and Law Enforcement about the current threat environment. Information sharing is critical to prevention, preparedness, and response.

HOMELAND SECURITY GRANT FUNDING

The FDNY cannot reinforce enough how critically important Federal funding has been in supporting the initiatives outlined above. Since 9/11, the FDNY has worked to build partnerships with key funders—notably the U.S. Department of Homeland Security (DHS) and the New York State Division of Homeland Security and Emergency Services (DHSES). To these agencies, we have communicated the FDNY's unique role in preparing for, responding to, and recovering from acts of terrorism, natural disasters, and other complex emergencies. To date, the FDNY has been awarded over $560 million in Federal funding through DHS.

The FDNY has utilized DHS funds to rebuild after 9/11 and to prepare our first responders to manage the potential threats and hazards they face each day in the field. Grant funds support the equipment, planning, drills, technology, and training they need to prepare for and respond to these threats.

An example is the Times Square Car Bomb. Through their training, first responders from Engine 54 and Ladder 4 immediately recognized the threat potential of the smoking vehicle. They took actions that day that reduced injuries, protected property, and saved lives.

During Super Storm Sandy, the FDNY fought devastating structural fires, responded to over 5,000 medical emergencies and rescued more than 500 residents. The FDNY was able to draw upon DHS-funded training and equipment during Super Storm Sandy operations.

A third example is the city's response to Ebola. In managing potential cases of EVD, the FDNY was able to draw upon a preparedness framework combining training, resources, and drills that specialized units developed preparing for Bio-Terrorism threats. This includes operating in chemical protective clothing, which as an added benefit, also protects against blood-borne pathogens. DHS funds helped build and train the HazTac and HazMat Units that played a key role in the response, and supported the purchase of specialized PPE and resources that provide emergency medical transport, treatment, and patient care.

By investing in core areas—planning, incident management, leadership, communications, patient triage and treatment, Haz-Mat, marine firefighting, and search and technical rescue—we are better prepared today when disaster strikes. These capabilities served the Department and the city during the Times Square incident, during Super Storm Sandy, the building collapses in East Harlem and Second Avenue, the response to Ebola, and during the train derailment along the Metro North commuter rail line.

These capabilities are a resource to the city, and when called upon, the entire New York region.

Again, I want to thank you for the opportunity to speak on these key topics, and reiterate that fire department resources can adapt to a changing threat environment. We have structured our core competencies to respond to routine and extreme events—including acts of terrorism.

Chairman MCCAUL. Thank you, Commissioner.
The Chair recognizes Mr. Ielpi.

STATEMENT OF LEE A. IELPI, PRESIDENT, SEPTEMBER 11TH FAMILIES ASSOCIATION

Mr. IELPI. Thank you, Mr. Chairman. Thank you, Committee. Thank you for inviting me here. It is a pleasure to be able to speak to you.

Before I start, I would like to acknowledge that behind me there is a large number of family members who lost their loved ones here that are here to listen to this talk today.

I would also like to thank the Port Authority Police Department behind me, who lost 37 fabulous guys and gals, 12 of which are still missing today; the New York City Police Department behind me, who lost 23, and 7 are still missing today; and, of course, the fire service, who lost 343, including my beautiful son Jonathan. Today, 127 New York City firefighters are still missing, along with 1,113 beautiful people who were murdered on 9/11 who are still missing this very minute.

I have listened to Mayor Giuliani and you folks who have done yeoman's work to keep us safe in this country of ours. I have had the privilege of going around the country; I have spoken in many cities and many States. I have actually traveled out of country, speaking about 9/11 and the importance of understanding what happened to our country, our world, on 9/11.

I spent 9 months here in recovery work. I worked with the best of the best that this country had to offer, not just the police, not just the fire department, emergency people, but our civilians from every one of your States, every one, that gave of themselves. They are now sick—sick. It is up to you, people of Congress, to speak up and support the Zadroga bill.

I heard many of you talk about the importance of making this a National memorial. It is critical we make this a National memorial. Your support to do that is instrumental in making this just that: The most powerful memorial this country has, the worst attack on our country's soil in history. It was not an attack on New York City or the Pentagon or Flight 93. It was an attack on Portland, Maine. It was an attack on Houston, Texas, and North Dakota. It was an attack on our soil, our beliefs, our lifestyles, our freedoms by people that do not believe that.

I listened to you talk about, and the commissioners, about how we protect ourselves, the police force, the military, and what we need to do. But I am very, very concerned that there is one thing that we have totally lacked in 14 years, and that is education. I can look at every one of you, every one of you, and we do not have a State in our country that I know of that has a curriculum to teach the history of what happened to us on 9/11—not a State. I find that very troubling.

We have teachers now that are 22, 23, 24, 25 years old that 14 years ago were 9, 10, 11, 12 years old, 13 years old. They went to school, and there is no curriculum. They weren't taught about 9/11. They don't know about 9/11, and now they are teachers.

When I tell you they don't know—I speak in these schools. I speak in these States. The last place I spoke was Omaha, a very large class of graduating students from high school who did not know about 9/11. The principal called me up, or emailed me, 3 or 4 days later and said, Lee, I have students walking in the hallways of this school asking about 9/11. What happened on 9/11? I have parents calling me up saying, "You don't teach 9/11? You don't educate our children about what happened to our country on 9/11?" The answer is no.

Just to drive that point home, a few days from now, on September 11, New York City schools do not have to have a moment of silence, nor do they have to talk about the significance of the day, unless the teacher wants to. So many of them do, but they are handcuffed. We teach to the test. You all know it. I spoke to teachers, again, throughout the country, and they have all said the same thing: We are failing our children.

Continue your beautiful work. You have to continue to keep us safe. But, please, when you go back to your individual States, your constituents, it is up to you to say to Michigan, to Texas, to California, "We don't have a curriculum in our State to teach what happened?"

We can fight these terrorists all day long. We know they are coming back. We hear it from our commissioners; we hear it from you. But wouldn't it be powerful to be able to say that our young people can take a stand with this by understanding, by enlightenment, by understanding that this terrorism factor is here to stay? One of biggest things that we were taught from our forefathers is education, and it will solve problems.

I will end—I spoke with an educator in London whose husband was murdered here. She went back to speak about, "We must educate here in the U.K., in London." This was a few years back. This is an individual, just one person. She came back and said to me, "Lee, I was told, no, we are not going to teach 9/11 in the United Kingdom. We do not want to aggravate the Muslim community."

I never heard such foolishness. We know there is more good Muslim people in this world, far more. But to be ignorant, that we are afraid to be politically incorrect is a downfall.

So we do have a lot of missions in our lives, don't we? I would sincerely—I would beg you, when you go to your States, ask that question. You are going to be very surprised with the answers you are going to get. "No, we don't teach it."

Thank you.

Chairman MCCAUL. Thank you, sir, for your passion and your advocacy for the victims.

The Chair recognizes Mr. Thomas.

STATEMENT OF GREGORY A. THOMAS, NATIONAL PRESIDENT, NATIONAL ORGANIZATION OF BLACK LAW ENFORCEMENT EXECUTIVES

Mr. THOMAS. Good morning, Chairman McCaul and the honorable Members of the House Committee on Homeland Security.

My name is Gregory Thomas. I am the national president of the National Organization of Black Law Enforcement Executives, commonly referred to as NOBLE. I am pleased to bring to you this morning testimony on behalf of our executive board and our over 3,000 members who we represent internationally, who are primarily African-American chief executive officers of law enforcement agencies at the Federal, State, county, and municipal levels.

Since 1976, we are proud to have served as a conscience of law enforcement by taking steps to ensure that there is equity in the administration of justice in all communities in the United States.

In response to the seminal events that occurred in our country over the past year, NOBLE is proud to have played a central role in our Nation's efforts to improve the level of respect between police and the citizens they serve. Whether by serving as a key member of President Barack Obama's task force on 21st-Century policing or working closely with the Department of Justice on the ground in Ferguson, Missouri, we have been an important part of the discourse that has sought to bring a fresh look to the manner in which police professionally engage with the communities that they serve and in a manner that communities respectfully engage with the police that serve them.

As steps are being taken by this honored committee to revisit importance lessons that have been learned in the post-9/11 world, NOBLE is pleased to present this committee with a view from the field on the levels of cooperation between Federal, State, and local law enforcement agencies in their joint efforts to prevent, prepare for, respond to, mitigate, and recover from a terrorist attack.

As we approach the 14th date of recognition, NOBLE would like to first offer its heartfelt condolences to the families of the over 3,000 people who lost their lives on September 11, 2001. We would like to also thank the men and women of all the public safety and law enforcement agencies and everyday citizens who gallantly responded to the sites of the terrorist attacks both here in New York City, in Pennsylvania, and at the Pentagon in Virginia.

The lessons learned from the September 11 attacks, a day which is commonly referred to as 9/11, are many. Arguably, the most important one is that there must be a unified intelligence-gathering effort always in place to ensure that we can properly identify plots and plans to attack our homeland and bring those who are behind these attacks to quick and determined justice.

Recent statements from FBI Director Comey that the Islamic State group known as ISIS, or ISIL, poses a more challenging terror threat within the United States than al-Qaeda does highlights the need for us to keep our collective eyes open for those who will choose to act in a singular manner to create terror, the likes of which was recently evidenced in a thwarted attempt in France.

This ever-present threat requires a top-level effort on the part of our Federal, State, and local law enforcement officials, an effort that will be greatly enhanced if these officials are given the structure to function properly.

Fortunately, since 9/11, there has been significant progress made in regards to information-sharing between agencies. But in order to achieve a more robust environment that actively promotes horizontal and vertical information sharing, NOBLE believes that properly-resourced intelligence fusion centers can serve a dual purpose of combating terrorism and fighting crime, therefore providing an excellent return on taxpayer investments.

In their 2006-issued guidelines on intelligence fusion centers, the Department of Justice defined a fusion center as a collaborative effort of two or more agencies that provides resources and information to the center with the goal of maximizing their ability to detect, prevent, investigate, and respond to criminal and terrorist activity.

Many of our members across the country either work in or have worked with these centers and, as such, have commented favorably about their ability to provide a forum wherein Government and private-sector entities can unite to maximize available resources, build trusted networks and relationships, and thoroughly investigate and prevent criminal and terrorist activity.

With some of our cities recently experiencing upticks in crime and with the general call for Government to do more with less, an expansion of these centers can serve to provide effective sources of timely intelligence related to violent gangs, drug trafficking, weapons smuggling, and other crimes that have a nexus to violence.

While fusion centers have a viable place in the law enforcement and intelligence communities, NOBLE strongly recommends that their work continue to be subject to periodic independent review and be held to high standards, like those previously established by the Department of Justice, for example, so as to minimize the chances of civil liberty or privacy abuses.

An example of a properly functioning and resourced fusion center can be found in Georgia, where in 2012 the Georgia Information Sharing and Analysis Center was named Fusion Center of the Year by the U.S. Department of Homeland Security.

In addition to creating and properly funding fusion centers, NOBLE also urges Congress to continue to support, create, and fund programs that ensure that equipment that was purchased shortly after 9/11—like those that were purchased, for example, to properly respond to chemical, biological, radiological, nuclear, and explosive threats, also known as CBRNE attacks—remain current and usable by our Nation's first responders.

Lastly, we also recommend that a strong emphasis be put on providing objective technical assistance and support for those agencies who want to apply for Homeland Security grants and assistance but, because of their size and financial capacity, have difficulty employing grant writers, for example, on a short- or long-term basis.

On behalf of the National Organization of Black Law Enforcement Executives, I thank you again for the opportunity to provide our views on this important and timely topic. I will remain and look forward to responding to your questions.

Thank you.

[The prepared statement of Mr. Thomas follows:]

PREPARED STATEMENT OF GREGORY A. THOMAS

SEPTEMBER 8, 2015

Good morning Chairman McCaul, Ranking Member Thompson, and the honored Members of the House Committee on Homeland Security. My name is Gregory Thomas and I am the national president of the National Organization of Black Law Enforcement Executives, commonly referred to as NOBLE. I am pleased to bring you testimony this morning on behalf of our executive board and over 3,000 members who we represent internationally, who are primarily African-American chief executive officers of law enforcement agencies at the Federal, State, county, and municipal levels. Since 1976, we are proud to have served as the "conscience of law enforcement" by taking steps to ensure that there is equity in the administration of justice to all communities in the United States.

In response to the seminal events in policing that have occurred in our country over the past year, NOBLE is proud to have played a central role in our Nation's efforts to improve the level of respect between police and the citizens they serve. Whether by serving as a key member of President Barack Obama's Task Force on 21st Century Policing or working closely with the United States Department of Justice and its Office of Community Oriented Policing on the ground in Ferguson, Missouri, we have been an important part of the discourse that sought to bring a fresh look to the manner in which police professionally engage with the communities that they serve and in the manner that communities respectfully engage with the police that serve them.

As steps are being taken by this honored committee to revisit important lessons that have been learned in the post-9/11 world, NOBLE is pleased to provide this committee with a "view from the field" on the levels of cooperation between Federal, State, and local law enforcement agencies in their joint efforts to prevent, prepare for, respond to, mitigate, and recover from a terrorist attack.

As we approach the 14th date of recognition, NOBLE would like to first offer its heartfelt condolences to the families of the over 3,000 people who lost their lives on September 11, 2001. We would like to also thank the men and women of all of the public safety and law enforcement agencies and everyday citizens who gallantly responded to the sites of the terrorist attacks both here in New York City, in Pennsylvania, and at the Pentagon in Virginia.

The lessons learned from the terrorist attacks from September 11, 2001, a day which is commonly referred to as 9/11, are many, but arguably the most important one is that there must be an unified intelligence-gathering effort always in place to ensure that we can properly identify plots and plans to attack our homeland and bring those who are behind these plans to quick and determined justice.

Recent statements from FBI Director Comey that The Islamic State group also known as ISIS or ISIL, poses a more challenging terror threat within the United States than al-Qaeda does, highlights the need for us to keep our collective eyes open for those who will choose to act "singularly" to create terror, the likes of which was recently evidenced in the thwarted attempt in France. This ever-present threat requires a top-level effort on the part of our Federal, State, and local law enforcement officials, an effort that will be greatly enhanced if these officials are given the structure to function properly.

Fortunately since 9/11, there has been significant progress made in regards to information sharing between agencies, but in order to achieve a robust environment that actively promotes horizontal and vertical information sharing, NOBLE believes that properly resourced intelligence fusion centers can serve a dual purpose of combatting terrorism and fighting crime, thereby providing an excellent return on taxpayer investments.

In their 2006 issued guidelines on intelligence fusion centers, the Department of Justice defined a fusion center as "a collaborative effort of two or more agencies that provide resources, [and] information to the center with the goal of maximizing their ability to detect, prevent, investigate and respond to criminal and terrorist activity".

Many of our members across the country either work in or have worked with these centers and as such have commented favorably about their ability to provide a forum wherein Governmental and private-sector entities can unite to maximize available resources, build trusted networks and relationships and thoroughly investigate and prevent criminal and terrorist activity,

With some of our cities recently experiencing upticks in crime, and with the general call for Government to accomplish more with less, an expansion of these centers can serve to provide effective sources of timely intelligence related to violent gangs, drug trafficking, weapons smuggling, and other crimes that can have a nexus to violence.

While fusion centers have a viable place in the law enforcement and intelligence communities, NOBLE strongly recommends that their work continue to be subject to periodic independent review and be held to high standards, like those previously established by the Department of Justice for example, so as to minimize the chances of civil liberty or privacy abuses. An example of a properly functioning and resourced fusion center can be found in Georgia where in 2012, the Georgia Information Sharing and Analysis Center was named Fusion Center of the Year by the U.S. Department of Homeland Security.

In addition to creating and properly funding fusion centers, NOBLE also urges Congress to continue to support, create, and fund grant programs to ensure that equipment that was purchased shortly after the 9/11 attacks, like those that were purchased for example to properly respond to Chemical, Biological, Radiological, Nuclear, and Explosive threats, (also known as CBRNE attacks) remain current and usable by our Nation's first responders.

Lastly, we also recommend that a strong emphasis be made on providing objective technical assistance and support for those agencies who want to apply for homeland security grants and assistance, but because of their size and financial capacity, have difficulty employing grant writers on a short- or long-term basis.

On behalf of the National Organization of Black Law Enforcement Executives, I thank you again for the opportunity to provide our views on this important and timely topic. I will remain and look forward to responding to your questions.

Chairman MCCAUL. I want to thank all the witnesses.

The Chair recognizes himself for questions.

Commissioner Bratton, you and I have talked a great deal about the evolving threat. You know, in the days of bin Laden, caves and couriers were used to communicate. It was a different type of threat, more of a command-and-control structure. But we see a threat today that—you talked about the Garland case, and you talked about the Fourth of July plot in New York, here.

Many of these new threats—we worry about foreign fighters, but many of these new threats are all internet-driven, coming out of places out of Syria by what we call the cyber, sort-of, ISIS commanders, if you will, sending out directives to attack military, to kill police officers.

You, sir, I think, have dealt with the majority of these threats. I think you mentioned in your testimony 20 plots have been thwarted just here in New York, and we have arrested over 60 in the last year. This is a threat that I believe is growing exponentially. It is a very different type of threat, more difficult to manage because of the sheer volume. It is loud. There is a lot of chatter—200,000 tweets, ISIS tweets, per day.

We did have a recent victory with the air strike against Junaid Hussain, al-Britani, who was sending many of these directives, sometimes with different Twitter handles, sometimes in dark space we can't even monitor even if we have a court order. We just, my understanding is, just recently now took out the No. 2 ISIS cyber recruiter. That is good news, but there will be many more to replace them.

So I guess my question is, and it is very challenging: What is NYPD doing, working with Federal partners, to rise to this challenge to protect the American people?

Let me just say, I commend you and your department for the great success you have had. But, again, the volume is so high, it worries me that we won't be able to stop all of this.

Mr. BRATTON. Your comment about the volume being so high reinforces the need for what New York has been very actively engaged in, and that is the collaborative effort with all of our various colleagues to ensure that we have seamless interaction with them.

It has been a trial-and-error process going back to the events immediately after 9/11. As chief in Los Angeles, along with many of my colleagues among the major city chiefs, we literally had to almost use a battering ram in Washington to break down the doors at Homeland Security to allow us into the room to share information and to share what we had.

Fortunately, those days are largely behind us, and, in New York City, I would like to think they are totally behind us, that, in this effort, there is too much to do to be bickering among ourselves or to be keeping information from each other.

My predecessor, Ray Kelly, in the days after 9/11 and in the 12 years he ran the NYPD, developed an extraordinary operation that not only would work with our Federal colleagues, which was an absolute necessity, but also because of the critical issues facing New York, being probably the most significant terrorist target remaining in the world today and continuing, created a very large and robust counterterrorism capability.

To that end, as the threats have changed, and particularly the last 18 months since my appointment as commissioner by Mayor de Blasio in January 2014, we have seen the threat of ISIS/ISIL expand exponentially with each passing month, using social media and also a strategy very different than al-Qaeda.

Al-Qaeda was focused on the big event, on multiple big events, which had been their practice. ISIL has gone in a very different direction, a direction that is really a 21st-Century initiative on their part, the idea that social media allows them to not only attract fighters to Syria but also inspire fighters elsewhere in the world, who don't have to be trained in training camps or experience warfare to conduct attacks.

You have referenced the 20 attacks that have been focused on New York City, 16 in 12 years thwarted by the NYPD, the FBI, and others. But the increasing pace, the idea that we have had 4 in just the last now 19 months, the pace is increasing because of that social media.

So we are going to continue to expand our response. We are going to continue to expand our proactivity. I referenced that just during my time as commissioner, with the additional resources Mayor de Blasio has been providing, 1,300 additional officers added to the department for the first time in 15 years—for 15 years, the size of the department was decreasing. It is now once again increasing.

A number of those officers are going into our Strategic Response Group, expanding from 400 to 800 officers. A large part of their mission will be to train for counterterrorism capabilities. Many of those officers are currently policing the U.S. Open, running all the security checkpoints that go into their facility.

Additionally, Commissioner Miller is creating a 415-person unit that will be very specifically focused on protecting sites here in New York City, specially equipped and armed to take the interim measure that was created by Commissioner Kelly and now institutionalize it because the nature of the threat we are facing has now become so big.

With reference to the issue of concern about cybersecurity, something whose full extent of potential harm we really don't fully understand—and I echo Mayor Giuliani's concerns that we are not doing enough there, but we are continually, with our resources in New York, trying to do more. Two-hundred-fifty detectives assigned to cybersecurity-related investigations a year or so ago, and recently the increase in assignment of personnel to the bureau as well as to District Attorney Vance's office.

So we are fully engaged and we are constantly looking at the exponential expansion of the threats and the new direction those threats are going.

Chairman MCCAUL. Well, I certainly commend you for your service. Thank you very much.

The Chair recognizes the Ranking Member.

Ms. SANCHEZ. Thank you, Mr. Chairman.

It is nice to have all of you gentlemen before us.

Commissioner Bratton, good to see you again. I used to work a little with you all up there in Los Angeles.

I am pretty thrilled that there are so many Members here today, especially some of our newer Members. So, in the interest of time, I have just one question, and it will go to the commissioner.

We have been investing a lot of resources. The resources that we have at the Federal level, of course, we have diligently worked to help New York City.

My question is: You are so far ahead in so many ways on this whole counterterrorism and how to deal with your communities and policing. How do you share that with some of the other cities, maybe some of the smaller cities that don't get those types of resources?

Mr. BRATTON. That is a great question. We consciously seek to take what we learn and share it. There is the major city chiefs organization, NOBLE that is here at the table, where continually throughout the year but then at our various annual conferences the issue of terrorism is now almost always a major topic of discussion at those roundtables.

Below the major city chiefs in most of the major cities of the country is the Intelligence Commanders Group, an entity formed right after 9/11. Los Angeles, when I was police chief there, led the way. Chief Michael Downing has become one of the more renowned experts on this issue. They meet continually to share information, not only in actual face-to-face meetings but through the various technologies available to us now. Then, in collaboration with IACP, National Sheriffs' Association, there is a lot more effort to keep them aware of changing tactics, techniques.

At the Homeland Security level, Homeland Security has evolved significantly under the leadership of the various Secretaries but particularly under Secretary Johnson. He has really made an effort to ensure that the various fusion centers, the various initiatives that have been undertaken, that we are true partners at the table, that there should be nobody below the salt, if you will, at our table, that all of us should be in a position to share.

That was not the case initially in 2002, 2003, 2004, when repeatedly we were banging on the door to be allowed in to even sit at the table, let alone be above the salt. Fortunately, a lot has changed, and we are continuing to improve our collaborative efforts.

Ms. SANCHEZ. Thank you, Commissioner.

I yield back, Mr. Chairman.

Mr. KING [presiding]. Thank you, Loretta.

First of all, I want to thank all the witnesses for being here today. Time is short, so I would like to focus on the whole issue of the Zadroga bill and 9/11 health care.

Before that, though, Commissioner Nigro, let me just commend Chief Joe Pfeifer for the great job that he has done. During the time that I was Chairman of the committee, Joe was extremely helpful to us, so I want to thank him for that and also for the tremendous heroism he showed on 9/11.

Lee Ielpi drove home the issue of the health care and the fact that people are dying to this day.

Dan, you and I over at Chief Ganci's funeral, I remember you spoke about 343 being killed. Well, since then, another 111, I think, have died directly from 9/11 health-related illnesses.

So I would like to ask Commissioner Nigro and Commissioner Bratton if they could just focus on the importance of extending the Zadroga bill.

Also, I would say parenthetically, I think every Presidential candidate should be obligated to take a stand on this issue, because this goes right to the heart of what America is all about.

So, Commissioner Nigro, since you suffered the most.

Mr. NIGRO. Well, certainly, the fire department's support for the Zadroga bill couldn't be stronger. As you stated, we might have thought on 9/11 that our losses ended with 343. We have added more than 100. This afternoon, we will add 21 names. The families of those 21 members will be at our headquarters as those names get added to our memorial wall.

I am sad to say that the memorial wall we created will soon be too small, because those losses continue to mount. We have 15,000 people registered, retired and active members, in the World Trade Center health program. We have more than 1,000 cases of cancer among those people. We have many sick members, retired and active, to take care of.

So the importance of this bill for us should go without saying but I will repeat it. I could not support it in a more strong fashion.

Mr. KING. Commissioner Bratton.

Mr. BRATTON. My comments would echo those of the commissioner, that, similarly, just during my time as commissioner, I have participated in a number of wakes and funerals for survivors of 9/11 but who did not ultimately survive the efforts that they put in at the pile and the illnesses that they contracted there.

This is a National obligation, a National debt, and it must be fulfilled.

Mr. KING. The bill expires this year, and the funding will run out by next year.

We have 35 seconds. Lee Ielpi, what can you tell us on Zadroga?

Mr. IELPI. I spent 9 months in recovery work, and I worked with the best of the best that this country had to offer. It is our obligation to support them.

The fire service, we have been very fortunate, but the underlying problem is the people that don't have this. They are not firefighters, PD. They are people that came here from all over the country. If we don't support them, what kind of a message are we sending out to the rest of this country of ours? They need help.

The major illnesses are cancers, respiratory, sinus, psychological problems. Those are the major ones; there are a lot more besides that. The psychological problems don't show themselves until it is manifested to the point where you realize that the person is having a severe problem—suicides, drug, marriage abuse problems.

We focus on them. We can find them because we keep track of them within the uniformed services. It is the people that don't have that support. We must endorse the Zadroga bill. It is critical for our country.

Mr. KING. Thank you, Lee, and thank you for your service.

Again, I would urge every Presidential candidate to come out on this issue.

With that, the gentlelady from Texas, Ms. Jackson Lee.

Ms. JACKSON LEE. Mr. Chairman, thank you so very much.

I am interested in making a little history here this morning, or this afternoon, and maybe draw upon this great committee to sign a letter to encourage the immediate placing of this legislation on the floor of the House to be voted on and to get it to the President's desk.

I want to thank Congressman King, Congresswoman Maloney, and Congressman Nadler, who have been leading on this, and all of us have joined them.

So I believe the message today, besides this being a very key hearing as we lead up to 9/11, is that we can leave no one behind, and certainly those who now live or those who have passed, tragically, since 9/11 because of the tragic impact of that devastating day.

Mr. Ielpi, let me say to you that the families will never be forgotten. I know what an emotional drain and experience that you have had, and thank you for your courage of going around to educate people. You have certainly given me a moment to raise the question: Why don't we have across America a moment of silence on that day or that we work with our students and our schools across America? So thank you for that. But I mourn the loss. It is a painful experience, and it is one that we feel deeply. I thank you so much for your presence here.

Let me quickly ask my questions to Commissioner Nigro, Mr. Thomas, and Mr. Ielpi. Let me see if I can get them all out, and then you all can answer them.

Commissioner, we committed ourselves on 9/11 to not let fear or terrorism cause us to terrorize ourselves. I would hope that you and Mr. Thomas could share in this, and that is, how the civilian police have to balance, to interact to do their duties, both in terms of law enforcement and fighting terror and dealing with a democratic society.

Mr. Nigro, if you would answer—as I came in, I could not avoid the powerful image of Ladder 3. I paused for a moment to read that story, which is the potent thing about what history is about, to know that that captain, I believe, had to use a landline, the one phone that was there, dealing with giving signals or messages down. God bless him. May he rest in peace. But the question of interoperability, if you would answer that question.

Last, Mr. Thomas, I want to thank you for bold leadership and ask you about the Law Enforcement Trust and Integrity Act that gives sort-of a roadmap for officers to continue to improve themselves as they serve us, but also the same question you might want to answer of interacting in a world where you are dealing with terrorism but also dealing with a democratic society.

I thank you all very much.

Commissioner Bratton. I asked you about the terrorism, but I will go to him first.

Mr. NIGRO. Certainly.

Ms. JACKSON LEE. Okay.

Mr. NIGRO. It is certainly a sad story about communications on 9/11 and the failures that day. I think the Department in the 14 years since has recognized those failures and identified each one and corrected the problems.

So, today, in today's world, we communicate with the other agencies, with the police department quite readily. We have the capacity to communicate with one another now from all floors of these buildings. Certainly, in the new One World Trade Center and the buildings around them, we have hardened communications that will sustain themselves.

But all of those sad facts of 9/11 and many other areas where we saw that we could improve, we have. Much of that is with the help of the Federal Government and funding that we have received.

Chairman MCCAUL [presiding]. If I could just interject, we have a hard stop at 1 o'clock to catch our train. So, in the interest of time so all of the Members can fully participate, I would like to move on and ask the Members to try to be as brief as possible.

Ms. JACKSON LEE. Mr. Chairman, if I could ask the witnesses to maybe provide the answers in writing and thank them again for——

Chairman MCCAUL. I thank that would be a good idea.

Ms. JACKSON LEE [continuing]. Their very astute presence here today. Thank you.

I yield back.

Chairman MCCAUL. I appreciate that. Thank you.

The Chair recognizes Mrs. Miller.

Mrs. MILLER. Thank you, Mr. Chairman.

In the interest of time, I am not sure I have a question but maybe a comment, particularly for Mr. Ielpi, who talked very eloquently about our lack of educational curriculum in all of our schools about what happened on 9/11 and why it happened and what this symbolizes here and the threats that our world and this new generation is facing, as well.

So, just listening to you, I emailed one of my staff here, saying, listen, I need to draft a letter to the Michigan State department board of education and ask them what kind of curriculum they actually have about 9/11. I intend to do that. It might be calling you later to ask you some thoughts on that.

But I think it is very, very important. Here we are 14 years later, and so many of these kids weren't born or were so young they don't really understand it. I think what is absolutely critical is the educational component to help them all understand it and how important it—what it really symbolizes and, again, how we keep ourselves safe and secure going forward. It is up to the next generation. It always is; that is just the way of the world.

Mr. IELPI. We have been saying this for years, that one of the ways to fight terrorism is to go at it full force, and one of those ways is through education, through enlightenment. If we continue down this road of political correctness, where we are afraid to say things, that is foolish, and the terrorists are laughing at us every time this subject comes up.

So thank you. I hope you can prove me wrong, but I know Michigan——

Mrs. MILLER. Yeah, I really am not aware. I hadn't really thought about it, to tell you the truth. So——

Mr. IELPI. I think we all——

Mrs. MILLER [continuing]. I think that is a good point.

Mr. IELPI [continuing]. Fall into that same subject, where we assume that our children are getting the correct education when they go to school, and then we find out that we are not. We spoke about this last night in our State.

Mrs. MILLER. Thank you very much.

I yield back.

Chairman MCCAUL. The Chair recognizes Mr. Vela.

Mr. VELA. Mr. Ielpi, thank you for bringing that to our attention. What I think we can do for you, there are five of us from the Texas delegation here, and we can get together, along with the other members of the Texas delegation, and write a letter to our Governor, talk to him and see what we can do about that. I think it is very important.

On the issue of the National museum, I think you and everybody else in New York can count on all of us here on the committee to support that effort, as well.

I do have questions with respect to the streamlining of your efforts, Commissioner, across the country. But, in the interest of time, I am going to yield my time so that our colleagues from the State of New York will have time to ask questions.

Chairman MCCAUL. I thank the gentleman.

The Chair recognizes Mr. Katko.

Mr. KATKO. Thank you, Mr. Chairman.

Thank you all for being here today.

I have had the pleasure of being in a secure briefing with Commissioner Bratton, and, upon speaking with him again last night and with Mr. Nigro, it is clear to me that New York is in excellent hands.

You are doing a great job fighting the war on terrorism and thinking outside the box, being innovative, and doing a wonderful job. So I simply want to commend you for that.

Mr. Ielpi, I had some wonderful conversations with you last night. I still can't imagine what it is like to lose a loved one in the manner in which you did. Then for you to have to carry your son's body out of the wreckage, it has to be—I know it is a life-altering thing for you.

For the other families that are here today, my heart bleeds for you, our hearts bleed for you.

You know, going through this memorial yesterday, I saw that adjacent to one wall here is where some of the remains are that have been unidentified, and behind in the coroner's office. I hope we can continue to support that effort.

But, with respect to education, I was horrified to learn of the lack of education and the lack of priority given to this. We learned as kids in school about World War I, World War II, the Vietnam war. This is a war on terror, and it is the greatest act of the war on terror ever perpetrated against us. It is our solemn duty to make sure that we never forget it, because, as we all know, we learn from history.

So, Mr. Ielpi, quickly, I would like to say, if you could wave a wand, what would you like to have happen to make sure that this education effort continues? What will be the best way to do it?

Mr. IELPI. I have 9 grandchildren. My buddy, my son, my oldest son—I have four children—gave his life that day. My wish would be that my grandchildren understand the sacrifices made not just by the people that were murdered on 9/11, the Pentagon, Shanksville, here, but the sacrifices that were made by our men and women in uniform since 9/11. That is why we are here; that is why this commission has been established.

That would be my wish, that I would leave this beautiful world of ours knowing that our children, our grandchildren are going to have that knowledge on how to make tomorrow that better day. It is our obligation to make tomorrow a better day, and that would be my wish.

Chairman MCCAUL. Mr. Hurd is recognized.

Mr. HURD. This is why we do field hearings, right? Learning about these issues.

Mr. Ielpi, I appreciate, you know, making us aware of these. Any information you have on people that are close to maybe getting it done or suggestions so that we are not starting from ground zero would be helpful for the entire committee. If you could submit that to us, that would be fantastic.

On the night at 2 o'clock a.m., the night after the airplane went into the Twin Towers, I was called by my boss and said, report to the basement of the old headquarters building in the CIA office. I became one of the first employees in the unit that ended up prosecuting the war in Afghanistan and bringing to justice some of those that did these dastardly deeds on our land.

It would be great if this is the last facility of its kind in the United States of America. If I were to engage my pessimistic side, I would say this is not going to be the last.

But when I think about the heroism that was displayed on that day, when I think about the number of men and women in the intelligence services and our diplomatic corps and our military and the men and women that you all represent on local law enforcement that are still operating as if it is September 12, 2001, it warms my heart and makes me think maybe this is going to be the last facility of its kind in the United States of America.

It is important. I remember what it was like in August in the CIA building, and there was concern, chatter: Something is going to happen, we don't know what it is. We weren't able to put the dots together. Knowing and then seeing what happened, those intelligence failures—you know, one of the reasons I ended up being where I am today was to see how I could help the intelligence community.

We alluded to it earlier, this idea of, instead of "need to know," moving to "need to share." It is hard to change cultures. That is what the intelligence community is based off of. Things have changed in a huge way, but I am interested to hear from you all, from the commissioners, what specific things can we be doing to get more intelligence in your hands to do your jobs?

Mr. BRATTON. I think we are doing it. I think, as I have referenced, as Mayor Giuliani before me referenced, that the collaborative efforts that have helped to inform us, to the extent of here in New York thwarting those 20 attempted attacks, around the country the increasing pace of attacks that are being constantly disrupted, it really is all about collaboration. It is about the idea of openness and transparency between the respective entities that are engaged in trying to keep our communities safe.

The good news is that we are evolving at a rapid pace in that regard and continuing to do so.

Mr. NIGRO. I think for the fire department—and I think Congressman King mentioned before Chief Joe Pfeifer, who runs our Center for Terrorism and Disaster Preparedness, works very closely with local and National law enforcement, keeping our members up-to-date, keeping situational awareness each and every day as if it is September 12.

The department has not forgotten. The department stays alert and stays ready. We appreciate the support that makes this possible, because these things take support. We have been getting support from the Federal Government. We need it to be sustained.

Mr. HURD. I yield back.

Mr. THOMAS. If I might, Mr. Chair——

Chairman MCCAUL. Yes. Sure.

Mr. THOMAS [continuing]. Just add one another thing too?

I mentioned again in my statement about the fusion centers. Their structure is robust enough to keep that flow of information going properly.

I wanted to add one other thing, one other sector that was very effective on that day, on 9/11. I was the director of security for New York City schools on that day. We had 8 schools near the Twin Towers here, 2 high schools about 20 yards south of the South Tower.

The collaboration on that day led to us rescuing 9,000 students and staff from those schools and nobody missing, killed, or injured, because the fire department and the police departments worked together beforehand, collaboration with fire drills and preparedness plans. On the day of the event, the fire department's response and the NYPD's response was important for us to have those children rescued.

So I would also say that it is important that the plans also include those areas of the government, mostly schools, who are designated as soft targets but are right in the realm of what can go on depending on where they are located in your respective States.

Chairman MCCAUL. Mr. Ratcliffe.

Mr. RATCLIFFE. Commissioner Bratton, as the Chairman of the Subcommittee on Cybersecurity, Infrastructure Protection, and Security Technologies, I wanted to ask you a little bit about ISIS. We have talked today about how they have effectively used social media in a way that al-Qaeda never did to essentially create terror franchises, to create a force multiplier of the disenfranchised in our society.

One of the problems with respect to that has been their effective use in using encrypted communications through social media. That has been a growing concern for law enforcement generally. FBI Director Comey has talked about it.

I wanted to give you an opportunity to talk about that publicly and comment in any way on how your police force is able to or is trying to mitigate the associated risks with that.

Mr. BRATTON. That is an excellent question. In this morning's *New York Times,* front-page story on just this issue, about the many aspects of it that are going to have to be addressed as we go forward.

I have met with the FBI director on a number of occasions on this issue, as recently as last week with District Attorney Cy Vance, the concerns about the encryption capabilities being built into so many of the devices that various companies, whether it is Google, Apple, and others, are marketing to their customers and how that is impacting, potentially, on our ability to investigate not only crime but terrorism.

But it is a Pandora's box of many issues, we have found as we have opened it, but we need to get into that box and sort it out, because it does impact greatly on our ability to investigate traditional crime, whether it is kidnappings and other forms of crime, or the growing, ever-growing area of terrorism, and impacts on our ability to track these people down once we, in fact, spot them on social media.

Mr. RATCLIFFE. Thank you, Commissioner.

I will yield back the balance of my time.

Chairman MCCAUL. The Chair recognizes Mr. Donovan.

Mr. DONOVAN. Thank you, Mr. Chairman.

Commissioner Bratton and Commissioner Nigro, I would just like to ask the same question to both of you.

When I was the district attorney of Staten Island for 12 years, there were certain things that I didn't want the public to know about how I spent my money. I didn't want people knowing what hotels we put witnesses in. The auditors had ways that we could account for the moneys that we spent but without revealing, for safety reasons, how we spent that money.

The Department of Homeland Security funding that you receive, are there ordered requirements, restrictions, things that hamper your ability to utilize that money in the best way that you could use it to protect the people of New York City?

Mr. BRATTON. One of the issues that we have discussed over a number of years with Homeland Security—and, in fact, you in Congress have some control over this—is the issue of when we spend the money and the time frame within which we spend it—that, by the time we get the authorization suspended, by the time we get the appropriate requests in, oftentimes there is a need to go beyond the requirements of the law as to within what time frame we have to spend it. You want to close the books.

It is an issue we have raised repeatedly. Hopefully, as you go forward, your efforts on this committee, to take a closer look at that still-unresolved issue.

We get, fortunately, a lot of money into New York City, and I certainly thank the Congressional delegation that leads those efforts. But it is the requirements in terms of how quickly we have to spend it. It takes quite a while to get the contracts up and running, and we spend it over a period of time.

So that is an issue of concern as it relates to funding mechanisms that we still experience.

Mr. NIGRO. I think Bill took the words right out of my mouth, because we are just recently experiencing the same issues. It is one thing, we can sometimes purchase things if they are items to purchase, but much of it is training. This training takes time and scheduled, and to try to fit it into a certain very specific time frame becomes very difficult. So we constantly run into that issue of spending the money within the assigned time, especially in the areas of training.

Mr. RATCLIFFE. I thank you both for being here today and for protecting my family.

I yield my time, Mr. Chairman.

Chairman MCCAUL. I thank the Members for being so efficient on time that we have a little extra time. I want to recognize Ms. Jackson Lee for her one follow-up question.

Ms. JACKSON LEE. Mr. Chairman, thank you. It was Mr. Thomas who did not get a chance to answer the question that I had given him.

As I do that, let me acknowledge one of my constituents, Deputy Darren Goforth, who lost his life tragically over the last week. We buried him last week. Certainly, it speaks to the difficulty of serving in law enforcement.

What I asked you, Mr. Thomas, was about the Law Enforcement Integrity Act, but to talk about that and the dual role that law enforcement have, of this issue of terrorism but also working in a civilian population, how they balance those responsibilities.

Thank you so much for all of your presence here.

Mr. THOMAS. Yes. Thank you.

Ms. JACKSON LEE. Thank you, Mr. Chairman.

Mr. THOMAS. So the Law Enforcement Trust and Integrity Act you are referring to, which NOBLE supports and endorses wholly, is one that is focusing on trying to improve the standards for law enforcement, that there will be some structure, that they will be focusing on how to conduct themselves in a very structured way.

Now, again, some police departments do that every day on a regular basis. Some have challenges doing that based on their numbers of personnel and budgets. But the act itself defines some standards that are easy to attain, standards that are similar to the ones that CALEA puts forth now, the Commission on Accreditation for Law Enforcement Agencies.

But, also, the act talks about youth reform and incarceration and talks about the need to look at how we sentence our youth. There are some youth who have, I guess, some events that are deviant that are not their doing per se but based on their mental state. The act, in itself, looks at that issue, particularly as it relates to those who are incarcerated for longer periods of time, as it relates to solitary confinement and the like.

Now, as it relates to the events that we are going through now over the past year in law enforcement that you referred to earlier, there is a challenge now for the law enforcement community generally to focus on the regular day-to-day issues of crime-fighting but also now adding on top of that terrorism and interweaving those together.

We know that the challenges that are out there now in the community are really few. There is a lot that is in media right now. Law enforcement is doing their job properly every day. It is more that we focus on the issues that they are doing right rather than wrong.

So any effort we have now to empower law enforcement better, with the ability to do better community policing and to have better training and have the appropriate staff—that is another issue, as well, because, since 9/11, staffing has waned in some police departments. Here in New York City, for example, the number has gone down. So it is important that we not lose the focus on making sure that we have the right amount of people staffed properly and properly trained.

Ms. JACKSON LEE. Mr. Chairman, thank you so very much.

I also want to thank Mayor de Blasio for his service and all of you who are here.

Thank you, Mr. Chairman. I yield back.

Chairman MCCAUL. The Chair recognizes Mr. King for a brief statement.

Mr. KING. I just—what Lee Ielpi did not say is that he suffered cancer from 9/11 and also still has two nodules on his lungs.

So hang in there, Lee.

Mr. IELPI. Thank you.

For those of you—I think the question was brought up before about curriculum. Our organization, which is the 9/11 Tribute Center—I am a board member of this organization, which I am so proud of what has been accomplished here. Our little organization, we give out a teacher award every year to teachers that go above and beyond, that talk about 9/11, teach 9/11.

We gave an award out 3 years ago to a teacher that came from Milford, Connecticut, and she received the award. When she came, she came with her principal and some of the other staff members from the school. When they went back to Milford, Connecticut, they wrote us and said, would you come and help us? We are thinking of putting together a curriculum for the school district of Milford, Connecticut.

Every State runs their educational system differently. In New York, it is regents folks. Milford, Connecticut, we went, we spoke. Last year, Milford, Connecticut, to the best of our knowledge, is the only school district in our country that has a written curriculum to teach the history of 9/11. They are not afraid to talk about who did this, why, and how do we make it better.

So, if you are interested, we are always in contact with our teachers. We will be able to supply their curriculum. I am not going to say it is the best in the world, but it is a start. So, if you are interested for your own States, Milford would be more than happy to assist you in any way they can.

Chairman MCCAUL. Let me thank the witnesses.

Let me close with this. I recently cosponsored the Zadroga Act, the 9/11 health care bill—I know Mr. King is one of the chief sponsors—and also the National 9/11 Memorial at the World Trade Center Act. It is our obligation, I think, and our duty, it is the responsibility of the Federal Government to do so.

Let me close with saying this. As with Pearl Harbor, the Kennedy assassination, I think everybody remembers where they were and what they were doing on September 11. I, for one, was with my 5-year-old, now 19-year-old, daughter watching the second plane fly into the second tower, realizing at that time as a Federal prosecutor that this was not some random act but rather a very cold, calculated act of terrorism.

I think it is incumbent, Mr. Ielpi, as you pointed out, that we never forget that day and that we teach the next generation of Americans the importance of what happened that day so that it never happens again.

So, with that, let me again thank the witnesses. It has been a very valuable hearing.

I want to thank again the museum for allowing us to conduct this hearing in a very historic setting. It has been a tremendous experience, and I want to thank everybody involved, including all the staff, who worked so hard to make this possible.

With that, this hearing now stands adjourned.

[Whereupon, at 12:30 p.m., the committee was adjourned.]

○